Hidden Spending

Hidden Spending

The Politics of Federal
Credit Programs

Dennis S. Ippolito

The University of North Carolina Press
Chapel Hill and London

Library of Congress Cataloging in Publication Data

Ippolito, Dennis S.

  Hidden spending.

  Includes bibliographical references and index.

  1. Government lending—United States. 2. Loans—

United States—Government guaranty. I. Title.

HJ8119.I65   1984   336.3   84-3652

ISBN 978-0-8078-1614-1 (cloth: alk. paper)

ISBN 978-0-8078-4121-1 (pbk. : alk. paper)

For Nancy Elizabeth

Contents

Preface xiii

Chapter 1
Spending, Credit, and the Budget 3

Chapter 2
Components of Federal Credit Activity 18

Chapter 3
Accounting for Federal Credit 43

Chapter 4
Credit without Controls 64

Chapter 5
The Credit Budget—Information versus Enforcement 90

Chapter 6
The Reagan Initiatives 106

Chapter 7
Controlling Federal Credit 130

Notes 149

Index 163

List of Tables

1.1 The Growth of Budget Outlays, Fiscal Years 1955–1982   6

1.2 Outstanding Federal Loans, Fiscal Years 1970–1982   6

1.3 Gross versus Net Lending, Fiscal Years 1980–1982   9

1.4 Unified and Actual Budget Deficits, Fiscal Years 1974–1982   10

1.5 Federal Participation in Domestic Credit Markets   11

1.6 Average Loan Terms and Comparable Market Interest Rates, Direct Loan Programs, by Agency, 1982   14

1.7 Average Loan Terms, Selected Loan Guarantee Programs, by Agency, 1981   14

2.1 Budget Shares, Defense versus Payments for Individuals, Fiscal Years 1955–1983   20

2.2 Human Resources Spending, Fiscal Years 1970–1985   21

2.3 Direct Loan Obligations and Loan Guarantee Commitments, by Function, Fiscal Years 1950–1982   24

2.4 Major Loan Guarantee Programs, Fiscal Year 1982   27

2.5 Major Direct Loan Programs, Fiscal Year 1982   35

3.1 Federal Financing Bank Holdings, Outstanding Agency Debt, Fiscal Years 1975–1983   57

3.2 Outstanding Federal Financing Bank Holdings, Agency Debt, Loan Assets, Direct Loans, Fiscal Years 1976–1983   57

3.3 FmHA Lending, Budget Balances, and CBO Sales to the FFB, Fiscal Years 1974–1983   60

3.4 Outlay and Deficit Understatements Caused by FFB Financing, Fiscal Years 1974–1983   62

4.1 Credit Legislation Enactments, by Functional Category, 1965–1982   66

4.2 Outstanding Credit Advanced by Government-Sponsored Enterprises, 1970–1982   68

4.3 Current and Previous Off-Budget Agencies   69

5.1 Net Federal Credit and Federal Credit Control, Fiscal Year
1981 Estimates   94

5.2 Appropriations Bill Limitations, Fiscal Year 1981 Estimates   95

5.3 Outstanding Federal Credit and Net Federal Credit, Fiscal
Years 1979–1981   96

5.4 House Budget Committee Credit Budget Recommendations,
Fiscal Year 1981   99

5.5 Federal Credit Outstanding, Fiscal Years 1979–1981   103

5.6 Direct Loans—Credit Budget versus Program Activity, Fiscal
Year 1981   103

5.7 Loan Guarantees—Credit Budget versus Program Activity,
Fiscal Year 1981   104

6.1 Reagan Administration and Congressional Spending and Credit
Budget Aggregates, Fiscal Years 1981–1986   108

6.2 Estimated and Actual Changes in New Lending, by Agency,
Fiscal Years 1980–1982   111

6.3 Reagan Administration Proposed Reductions in Credit
Programs, Fiscal Years 1984–1988   116

6.4 Action Required to Effect Major Program Reductions, Reagan
Fiscal 1984 Credit Budget   117

6.5 Estimated Outlay Impact of Reagan Credit Budget Proposals,
Fiscal Years 1984–1988   119

6.6 Reagan Administration and Congressional Credit Budgets, by
Function, Fiscal Year 1983   124

7.1 Interest Subsidy Values, Selected Direct Loan Programs, 1983   141

List of Figures

1.1 Net Federal Credit, Fiscal Years 1972–1988   8

2.1 Composition of the Spending Budget, Fiscal Years 1980–1985   22

2.2 Composition of Federal Spending and Federal Lending, Fiscal Year 1982   25

2.3 Total Guarantees Outstanding for Actuarially Sound Programs and for Programs for Marginal Borrowers   30

2.4 Federal Aid to Students for Higher Education, Fiscal Years 1971–1983   32

3.1 Net Lending and Loans Outstanding of the Federal Financing Bank, Fiscal Years 1974–1983   55

3.2 Direct Loan Disbursements, Farmers Home Administration, Fiscal Years 1951–1985   59

Preface

Each year, federal agencies distribute tens of billions of dollars in direct loans and guaranteed loans through a variety of credit assistance programs. There is disagreement about the effectiveness of many of these programs. There is also a good deal of uncertainty, and even growing apprehension, about their economic impact. While this book discusses the programmatic and macroeconomic issues associated with federal credit activity, its focus is on the political implications of credit.

The budgetary treatment of federal credit programs has exacerbated spending-control problems in Congress and the executive branch. Since the volume and, more important, the subsidy costs of federal credit assistance are not accurately reflected in the unified budget, credit programs are not forced to compete with direct spending or even with tax preferences. When pressures develop to control budget totals, as has been the case in recent years, credit programs offer a loophole. Substantial amounts of financial assistance can be distributed to a wide range of borrowers with little or no direct budgetary costs.

The loophole is deliberate. The budgetary distortions and evasions relating to federal credit accounting are the products of design, not accident. They have been used to shelter programs that otherwise could not compete successfully for scarce resources. They have served to protect credit programs from critical oversight. They have, until recently, frustrated attempts to direct congressional attention toward the growth and impact of credit policy.

In the absence of external controls, such as constitutional limits, fiscal discipline is heavily dependent upon appropriate norms and procedures. In practical terms, this means—at a minimum—comprehensive budgets and centralized spending control. Credit programs have eroded the comprehensiveness of the federal budget and weakened still further centralized control over spending. Under these conditions the prospects for fiscal responsibility are dim. This is especially true in Congress, which has typically found it difficult to resist spending pressures.

For much of our history the fiscal test applied to political institutions was simple. Budgets should, under normal conditions, be balanced. Deficits should, if unavoidable, be temporary. The norm of the balanced budget reflected certain beliefs about government and the economy, but it was influenced to a considerably greater degree by political assumptions. So long as spending had to be financed directly and immediately by taxation, the political benefits of spending would be offset by the political costs of taxation. Given the public's natural antipathy toward taxes, balanced budgets meant limited budgets.

This norm, however, no longer applies to the federal government. The federal budget has become an instrument of economic management. Whether it is balanced—which has occurred only four times in the past thirty years—is not considered a test of political virtue or economic desirability. There is, then, a different fiscal test, with budgets evaluated for their economic impact. As is now quite apparent, this impact is much too uncertain to guide political decision making. Cutting the nexus between spending and taxation, and not substituting a clear-cut standard for evaluating fiscal decisions, simply biases the political process toward increased spending and deficits.

A similar bias affects credit programs. It is not possible to predict the economic effects of credit programs or "credit budgets" with great confidence. Political judgments about credit programs, therefore, are insulated from macroeconomic constraints. Credit programs may, of course, sometimes be preferable to direct spending. But without a consensus on economic impact (which does not exist and is unlikely to develop) *or* information about budgetary costs (which could be made available), credit is likely to be chosen for budgetary rather than programmatic reasons. Moreover, the only constraint is occasional disquiet when credit totals grow very rapidly and interest rates increase.

This book, then, examines the relationship between fiscal realities and the political process. It will, I hope, illuminate that relationship and improve our understanding of not only credit programs but also fiscal decision making.

I have incurred many debts during the course of this study and would like to acknowledge at least some of them. Leslie Lenkowsky provided truly indispensable assistance. Professor Aaron Wildavsky contributed encouragement and insight as part of a comprehensive critique. A second, anonymous reviewer permitted me to benefit from a formidable expertise about credit programs. Karen Bussell was an integral and invaluable part of this project from beginning to end.

Hidden Spending

Chapter 1

Spending, Credit, and the Budget

Political controversies over the size, composition, and economic effects of the federal budget have greatly intensified over the past decade. Despite presidential and congressional efforts to restrain spending, budget growth has been rapid and seemingly uncontrollable, and deficits have reached unprecedented levels. Pressures to reduce spending growth and deficits have heightened the competition between budget priorities, particularly between defense and social welfare spending.

While the travails of the "official" budget have received a good deal of critical attention, direct spending and the fiscal policies necessary to finance this spending are only part of the current fiscal dilemma. Since the early 1970s, federal credit programs have proliferated and expanded dramatically and now represent an important, though largely hidden, form of government spending.[1] These programs are a principal component of federal policy in a number of areas—housing, agriculture, education, and international affairs—and have important economic consequences as well.

In fiscal 1972 the amount of federal and federally assisted credit outstanding was approximately $200 billion.[2] Ten years later, the total was well over $500 billion, and "one of every eight dollars extended by federal agencies was in the form of a direct loan or loan guarantee."[3] There are perhaps as many as 350 direct loan and loan guarantee programs.[4] Funds advanced through these and other federal sources account for more than one-fifth of the total funds advanced in U.S. credit markets.[5]

Both the Carter and Reagan administrations have attempted to bring federal credit activities under the umbrella of broader budget control efforts. In his fiscal 1981 budget, President Carter initiated a credit budget designed to focus greater attention on the use and economic impact of federal credit programs.[6] Two years later, the Reagan administration announced that "rigorous control over Federal credit programs . . . is an important part of the President's budget reform plan."[7] Congress has also begun to address problems of credit control and to explore means of integrating credit into the budget process.

Like spending programs, however, federal credit programs are inherently difficult to control, for they provide well-defined and substantial benefits to important constituencies. The desire for fiscal restraint thus collides with political pressures to maintain and even to expand individual programs. And unlike the spending budget, the costs of many credit programs are diffused and largely hidden. As one critic has pointed out, credit programs permit government "to claim that wonder of wonders—something for nothing, or almost nothing."[8] The claim is spurious, but it presents an extraordinary test of the fiscal responsibility of political institutions.

How Spending Is Hidden

The economic impact of federal credit programs extends to the allocation of credit, the composition of the economy, and, ultimately, the productivity and economic growth of the nation. The expansion of federal credit activity, however, is not reflected in the spending and deficit totals in annual federal budgets.

Most direct loans, which require immediate commitments of funds, are charged to off-budget agencies, while the budgetary consequences of guaranteed loans become apparent only in the case of default, when agencies must actually provide funds to repay lenders holding the guarantees.[9] Loan guarantees are by far the single largest category of federal credit activity, with the government's contingent liability exceeding $550 billion.[10] A wide range of borrowers thus receives assistance with little or no direct spending and, hence, no apparent budgetary costs.

There are other, less obvious, dimensions to the hidden costs of federal credit activities. All credit programs include subsidies, since borrowers receive assistance at lower interest rates or under more favorable conditions than would be available in private credit markets. Indeed, the element of subsidy is the principal reason for utilizing government rather than private credit. Lower interest rates, longer loan maturities, and related forms of favored treatment lower the costs of borrowing. The effective result is a cash grant to the borrower.

The precise cost of such subsidies, however, is often difficult to calculate and, in any case, is usually not translated into direct spending. When direct loans, for example, are extended at rates below prevailing market conditions (or even the interest rates the government pays to finance its own borrowing), their true costs are not reflected in the actual cash transactions, even when these transactions are handled by on-budget agencies.

The obscuring of costs is even more evident with loan guarantees. Federal guarantees typically allow borrowers to obtain funds at lower rates by eliminating the risk to lenders. They also affect the allocation and supply of credit. Loan guarantees thus have direct costs for nonassisted borrowers, in addition to direct benefits for assisted borrowers, but these costs are not reflected in budget outlays.

Guaranteed loans for individuals (such as students), corporations (such as Chrysler), and governments (such as New York City) or direct loans for housing, agriculture, and other purposes share a salient characteristic. They allow the federal government to extend financial assistance while minimizing or even eliminating budgetary costs. Subsidies in the form of direct grants would often serve essentially the same purposes as credit programs, but would have the disadvantage (for political officeholders) of driving up budget totals. Hidden spending allows legislators and executive branch officials to capitalize on the political benefits of distributing assistance while they escape the political costs of raising and financing budgets.

The Growth of Credit Activity

Since the mid-1970s the spending side of the federal budget has risen sharply, from less than $365 billion in fiscal 1976 to over $725 billion in fiscal 1982. Spending growth for this period averaged over 13 percent annually, well above the rate of spending increase during the preceding two decades (see Table 1.1). Spending has also continued to outpace economic growth, rising from an average level of less than 21 percent of gross national product during the 1970s to approximately 23 percent in fiscal years 1980–82.

While the spending budget illustrates the substantial, and growing, impact of federal fiscal activities on the economy, the inclusion of credit activities provides a much fuller and more accurate representation of this relationship. The expansion of federal credit activity has paralleled the remarkable rise in federal spending. By some measures, it has actually been more dramatic.

Measuring Credit Activity

There are various ways to measure federal credit activity. One of the more meaningful is the level of outstanding, or unpaid, loans at the end of a fiscal year. In 1970 this total stood at less than $180 billion, and it rose modestly over the next several years. The growth in credit programs then began to accelerate, resulting in annual increases that averaged almost 13 percent in the level of outstanding direct loans and loan guarantees between 1976 and 1982 (see Table 1.2).

The rapid growth in outstanding loan balances presages problems in the area of government liabilities. The Congressional Budget Office has esti-

Table 1.1 The Growth of Budget Outlays, Fiscal Years 1955–1982

Period	Average Annual Increase (percentage)
FY 1955–59	5.5
FY 1960–64	5.2
FY 1965–69	9.3
FY 1970–74	7.8
FY 1975–82	13.3

Source: *Budget of the United States Government, Fiscal Year 1984* (Washington, D.C.: Government Printing Office, 1983), p. 9-55.

Table 1.2 Outstanding Federal Loans, Fiscal Years 1970–1982 (in billions of dollars)

Fiscal Year	Direct Loans	Loan Guarantees	Total	Percentage Increase
1970	$ 51.1	$125.1	$176.2	—
1971	53.1	140.1	193.2	9.6
1972	50.1	158.9	209.0	8.2
1973	43.9	174.1	218.0	4.3
1974	61.5	153.2	214.7	−1.5
1975[a]	74.1	158.7	232.8	8.4
1976	85.9	169.8	255.7	9.8
1977	100.9	183.9	284.8	11.4
1978	120.4	226.1	346.5	21.7
1979	140.5	264.6	405.1	16.9
1980	163.9	298.5	462.4	14.1
1981	185.0	309.0	494.0	6.8
1982[b]	207.8	331.2	539.0	9.1
1983	223.0	363.8	586.6	8.9

Source: *Special Analysis, Federal Credit Programs, Budget of the United States Government,* Fiscal Years 1972–85.

a. Average increase, 1970–75 = 5.8 percent.
b. Average increase, 1976–82 = 12.8 percent.

mated that perhaps 95 percent of outstanding loans will ultimately be repaid, but this is admittedly based upon experience with older, established loan programs.[11] Data on defaults for many of the newer programs are limited and inconclusive, but there are indications that default rates may be substantially higher than those experienced in the past. In addition, some of these programs differ from traditional ones in that they are not protected by government claims on marketable property.

As shown in Figure 1.1, the volume of net federal credit extended each year—new direct loans and loan guarantees minus repayments—roughly tripled between 1972 and 1982, the major increases occurring in off-budget lending and loan guarantees. The budgetary impact of this growth, however, was restricted to the relatively stable net outlays of on-budget agencies.

Moreover, the use of net-lending figures gives a greatly reduced picture of federal credit activity because of the unusual accounting devices utilized by federal agencies. It is perfectly reasonable, for example, to deduct repayments of old loans from new loan commitments in order to measure an agency's net lending during a given fiscal year. These repayments, however, need not be made by the borrowers to whom the loans were extended. Instead, agencies are permitted to "sell" their direct loan obligations to the Federal Financing Bank (FFB).[12] When certain agencies sell loan obligations to the FFB, the sales are treated as repayments. On-budget direct loans are converted into off-budget loans, and this conversion allows agencies to add the new funds gained by loan sales to their appropriated funds. In 1981, for example, the Farmers Home Administration (FmHA) extended more than $9 billion in new direct loans for its agricultural credit program, but the net outlays for the program showed repayments exceeding new loans by some $900 million. This apparently negative loan activity was misleading, since almost $7 billion in supposed repayments was actually nothing more than the sale of loans to the FFB. The FmHA was repaid for its loans; the government was not. The on-budget loans, however, were now off-budget loans, and the FmHA was able to use its loan asset sales to make new loans. Through loan asset sales to the FFB by the FmHA and other on-budget agencies in 1981, over $14 billion in outlays was removed from budget totals, with a corresponding reduction in the reported unified budget deficit.

The accuracy of net-lending figures is further distorted by the treatment of defaults. In many cases, losses are covered by insurance or reserve accounts, with subsequent transfers to an agency's lending budget. This gives defaults the appearance of repayments in an agency's loan account.[13]

In order to provide a more accurate picture of program levels, the credit

Figure 1.1 Net Federal Credit, Fiscal Years 1972–1988

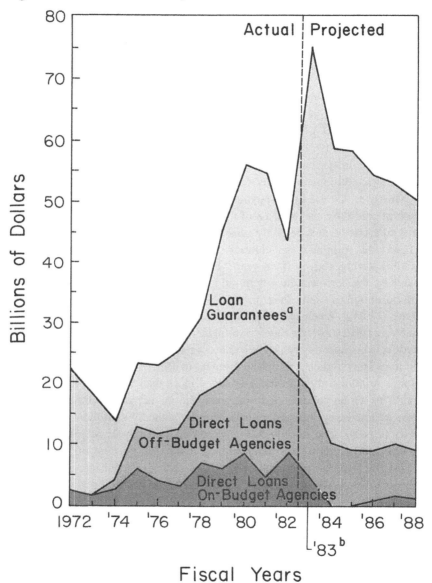

Source: Congressional Budget Office, *An Analysis of the President's Credit Budget for Fiscal Year 1984* (Washington, D.C.: Congressional Budget Office, 1983), p. 36.

   a. Primary guarantees: excluding secondary guarantees and guaranteed loans acquired by on- and off-budget agencies.

   b. Estimate.

budget format introduced in the fiscal 1981 budget reports gross levels of credit activity. The distinction is a major one. In fiscal years 1980–82, net direct lending averaged less than $25 billion annually (see Table 1.3). (The net lending outlays of on-budget agencies for these years averaged just under $8 billion.) The level of new direct loan obligations, however, was well over $50 billion annually. New guaranteed loans were also several times greater than the net change in outstanding guarantees.

The bulk of credit activity, then, is carried on outside the budget reported to the public. The budget is a cash-flow document. It does not show the volume of loan guarantees or the government's growing liability. The direct loan activities of on-budget agencies, which do require outlays, are grossly understated in the budget by the conversion of on-budget loans to off-budget loans and, to a lesser extent, by the accounting used to treat defaults.

The Real Deficit

Whether agencies are on-budget or off-budget, the government must still obtain funds to cover their lending programs. Under current circumstances, this is done by additional borrowing, which inflates the size of the annual deficit and the total federal debt. The actual deficits in recent years have been $10–20 billion higher than those reported in the unified budget as a consequence of off-budget credit spending (see Table 1.4). The result has been to add more than $100 billion to the federal debt.[14] This exceeds by more than $30 billion

Table 1.3 Gross versus Net Lending, Fiscal Years 1980–1982 (in billions of dollars)

	Fiscal Year			
	1980	1981	1982	Totals
New direct loan obligations	$51.1	$57.2	$54.9[a]	$163.2
Net direct lending[b]	23.4	21.1	22.8	67.3
New guaranteed loan commitments (primary)	82.2	76.5	53.7	212.4
Net guaranteed lending[b]	33.9	10.5	22.2	66.6

Source: *Special Analysis, Federal Credit Programs, Budget of the United States Government, Fiscal Years 1982–84.*

a. Starting with the fiscal 1984 budget, the Reagan administration subtracted loan asset repurchases from total new direct loan obligations. These repurchases ($7.4 billion for FY 1982) have been included here to provide comparability with previous years.

b. The net figure is based on the year-to-year change in outstanding loans or loan guarantees.

Table 1.4 Unified and Actual Budget Deficits, Fiscal Years 1974–1982 (in billions of dollars)

Fiscal Year	Unified Budget Deficit	Off-Budget Outlays	Actual Deficit
1974	$ 4.7	$ 1.4	$ 6.1
1975	45.1	8.1	53.2
1976	66.4	7.3	73.7
1977	44.9	8.7	53.6
1978	48.8	10.3	59.2
1979	27.7	12.5	40.2
1980	59.6	14.2	73.8
1981	57.9	21.0	78.9
1982	110.6	17.3	127.9
Total	465.7	100.8	566.6

Source: *Budget of the United States Government, Fiscal Year 1984* (Washington, D.C.: Government Printing Office, 1983), p. 9-55.

the combined budget deficits registered during the 1950s and 1960s,[15] and it substantially escalates, of course, the costs of interest payments on the federal debt.

Despite congressional and presidential professions of concern about the persistence and size of deficits, off-budget spending represents a budgetary evasion of considerable magnitude. As long as this fiction is allowed to continue, claims about fiscal responsibility deserve to be treated with some skepticism. At the same time, political pressures to produce more palatable deficits in the unified budget have made it difficult for Congress and the executive branch to incorporate off-budget agencies into spending budget totals.

Lending and Borrowing

The lending and borrowing activities of the federal government can also be assessed by focusing on the federal participation rates in domestic credit markets. These rates relate federal extensions of credit and federal borrowing to the total funds advanced or raised in U.S. credit markets. Total credit increased by approximately 335 percent between 1970 and 1982. Federal lending and borrowing, however, grew even more rapidly. The federal participation rate on the lending side rose from an average rate of about 14 percent during the 1970s to over 21 percent in the fiscal 1980–82 period. On the borrowing side, the federal participation rate went up substantially, from less than 20 percent in 1970 to almost 50 percent in 1982 (see Table 1.5). By the early 1980s, then, more than one out of every five dollars advanced in U.S. credit markets was being extended under federal auspices. Of the total funds raised, almost one dollar in two was necessary to cover the borrowing activities of the federal government.

The Costs of Hidden Spending

The introduction of an annual credit budget has provided greater information about the extent of federal credit activity, but data on costs (or benefits) remain inadequate. Since similar uncertainties regarding benefits apply to conventional spending programs, the major distinction between spending and lending involves their budgetary costs. Spending programs are measured as budget outlays, allowing comparability between programs and a reasonably accurate standard for assessing possible program changes. For a variety of

Table 1.5 Federal Participation in Domestic Credit Markets

Fiscal Year	Total Funds Advanced or Raised in U.S. Credit Markets (in billions of dollars)	Percentage Advanced under Federal Auspices[a]	Percentage Raised under Federal Auspices[a]
1970	93.6	17.2	19.1
1971	125.7	13.1	26.6
1972	151.9	14.5	25.7
1973	198.2	13.2	23.5
1974	187.5	13.6	12.9
1975	177.9	15.2	36.4
1976	243.1	11.1	40.4
1977	308.3	11.9	25.6
1978	383.4	15.2	24.5
1979	426.4	17.1	18.9
1980	366.4	21.8	33.7
1981	427.2	20.2	33.3
1982	408.7	21.4	48.9

Source: *Special Analysis, Federal Credit Programs, Budget of the United States Government,* Fiscal Years 1981–84.

a. Includes government-sponsored enterprises.

reasons, correspondingly precise standards do not exist for many lending programs. Two obvious indicators—defaults and interest subsidies—could be used to assess retrospective and prospective costs, but data about both are surprisingly incomplete. As one recent study concluded, "Defaults are rarely stated as a percentage of loan volume, interest costs are inadequately tied to interest payments, and losses associated with delinquency are almost indecipherable."[16]

Defaults

While overall default rates for direct loans and loan guarantees have been relatively low in the past, there is concern this may be changing. Defaults on student loans, which are unsecured, are considerably higher than anticipated. Guarantees on loans to certain foreign governments are causing problems. The federal government has guaranteed an estimated $600 million in loans by American banks to Poland, for example, and in January 1981, the Reagan administration was forced to pay over $70 million to forestall a default. There are indications that deferred payments and rescheduling of debts are being routinely used by some agencies to avoid defaults. A study of the Small Business Administration loan program found that almost 10 percent of new loans were being used to pay off previous loans and estimated that 10–25 percent of the SBA's loan portfolio was delinquent at any given time.[17]

The Office of Management and Budget (OMB), which has examined loan-servicing practices among federal agencies, reports that "payment deferrals are granted liberally" and rescheduling of debt "often becomes a routine practice rather than the exception."[18] Moreover, it appears that penalties for delinquent payments are rarely assessed; when such penalties are assessed, they are typically based upon subsidized interest rates. According to OMB, the lax standards employed by many lending agencies provide borrowers with "little or no incentive to make timely payments."[19]

Private lenders can use a borrower's credit rating as a means to encourage full and timely payments. Because of possible privacy restrictions governing the reporting of data on delinquencies and defaults, government agencies have been less likely to penalize borrowers in this fashion, although recent legislation has attempted to remove this obstacle.[20] The loan-servicing practices associated with government lending, then, represent an additional subsidy, since financial and non-financial penalties are less likely to be invoked against borrowers than would be the case with private lenders. Moreover, since some of the newer programs feature unsecured loans, losses resulting from delinquency and default may become a much more serious problem.

Interest Subsidies

The most important form of subsidy, however, is the lower interest charged for government loans compared to interest rates in the private sector or even the costs of the government's own borrowing. Interest rates and loan maturities vary widely among government credit programs. Depending upon the agency and program, direct loans may be extended for periods ranging from several months to forty years; interest rates differ as well, but they are typically well below comparable rates in private credit markets (see Table 1.6). Long loan maturities and relatively low interest rates are also characteristic of loan guarantee programs (see Table 1.7).

When a federally assisted borrower obtains funds at interest rates below those charged by private lenders, the federal government is providing a subsidy equal to the interest rate differential on the loan principal for each year the loan is outstanding. As might be expected, the extent of this subsidy affects the demand for credit assistance. In examining the loan program of the Federal Housing Administration (FHA), the General Accounting Office found "a statistically valid, direct relationship between the level of subsidy and FHA mortgage commitments." [21] The GAO concluded that benefit levels in the form of interest subsidies were likely to affect credit demand in other programs in a similar fashion.

Despite the importance of interest rate subsidies, OMB analysts acknowledge "there is no generally accepted method for quantifying the present value of interest subsidies in Federal credit programs." [22] For many programs, a comparable private rate cannot be estimated. In some instances, federal assistance is extended to borrowers and projects that are riskier than private markets would accept under any terms. In the 1981 budget OMB simply utilized a general comparability rate of 13 percent to produce a rough estimate of the subsidies involved with major direct loans and loan guarantee programs. For fiscal years 1979–81 the OMB reported that the values of interest rate subsidies averaged more than $26 billion annually. [23] Recent estimates utilizing comparable private market rates put the average annual subsidy costs of direct loans at approximately $10 billion for 1982–84, while the guaranteed student loan program alone is estimated as having an annual subsidy value of more than $2 billion. [24] The explicit, direct subsidies of federal credit programs, then, are quite substantial.

For direct loans the explicit subsidies involved (ignoring the implicit subsidies associated with the government's assumption of risks) are directly translated into taxpayer costs. This is obvious in cases where the government provides funds to borrowers at rates below its own borrowing costs. The subsidy

Table 1.6 Average Loan Terms and Comparable Market Interest Rates, Direct Loan Programs, by Agency, 1982

Department or Agency	Range of Average Loan Terms		Comparable Market Interest Rates[a] (percentage)
	Years	Interest Rates (percentage)	
President (economic support, development assistance, military sales)	15–40	2.8–10.5	12.5
Agriculture	<1–40	3.0–11.1	12.2–14.5
Education	7–30	3.0–7.5	13.4–18.0
Export-Import Bank	12	11.0	15.5
Health and Human Services	20	12.0	15.5
Housing and Urban Development	<1–40	3.0–10.0	12.5–14.5
Small Business Administration	8.5–9.0	11.5–14.5	15.5
Transportation	10–20.2	3.4–3.5	10.6–14.7
Veterans Administration	29–30	10.9–12.0	13.0–14.5

Source: *Special Analysis F, Federal Credit Programs, Budget of the United States Government, Fiscal Year 1984* (Washington, D.C.: Government Printing Office, 1983), pp. F-57–F-58.
   a. Private sector loan rates estimated for comparable programs, relying on broad categories of loan types.

Table 1.7 Average Loan Terms, Selected Loan Guarantee Programs, by Agency, 1981

Department or Agency	Average Loan Terms	
	Years	Interest Rates
Education	13.0	7.0
Health and Human Services	13.0	12.0
Housing and Urban Development	31.0	0.0
Interior	10.0	7.3
Small Business Administration	20.0	6.0

Source: *Special Analysis F, Federal Credit Programs, Budget of the United States Government, Fiscal Year 1982* (Washington, D.C.: Government Printing Office, 1981), p. 193.

to the borrower, however, is greater than this differential, since it amounts to the difference between the interest rate charged by government and the rate that would otherwise be charged by a private lender. This "additional subsidy" is not a direct taxpayer cost, but the increased borrowing demand may be reflected in higher interest rates for nonassisted borrowers. This is also true for guaranteed loans that, with the exception of default losses, appear to be cost-free for taxpayers. Like direct borrowing, guaranteed lending affects private credit markets and exerts similar upward pressure on interest rates. In addition, there are administrative costs associated with loan guarantee programs, and these are often considerable.

Economic Effects

In addition to their subsidy costs, federal credit programs also may have a broader—and in some cases negative—impact on the economy. Government intervention in credit markets alters the calculation of return and risk that would otherwise govern the flow of credit to potential borrowers. In effect, political judgments are substituted for private market assessments of return and risk in the allocation of credit.

With direct loans this works in a straightforward fashion. The federal government, which enjoys premier status in credit markets, borrows money and then lends it to borrowers who either might not be able to borrow in private markets or would be forced to pay higher interest rates. The result of this may be to "crowd out" nonassisted borrowers or at least to raise their interest costs, and it then becomes a matter of some importance whether assisted borrowers will use these funds more or less productively. If resources are in fact diverted from more productive to less productive uses, the efficiency of the nation's capital stock is diminished, resulting in lower rates of economic growth.

Loan guarantees can have similar reallocative effects. By assuming most or all of the default risk, the government can direct credit to favored borrowers. Again, this may involve not only lower interest rates but also access to credit for borrowers otherwise considered too risky to qualify. The element of risk is not eliminated, of course, but rather shifted from lenders to taxpayers. Crowding out can occur here as well, depending on the elasticity of credit, with risky borrowers replacing less risky but nonguaranteed borrowers. This can affect productivity and economic growth, depending upon the supported and unsupported activities involved, and the likelihood of a significant impact obviously increases as the volume and types of loan guarantee programs expand.

An additional consideration is the effect of federal credit activity on economic stabilization efforts. Many analysts argue that in order to facilitate economic stability, the levels of subsidy and program activity associated with federal credit assistance should run counter to the level of economic activity and be consistent with fiscal and monetary policy. This generally accepted prescription has usually not been followed. During the 1960s and 1970s federal credit assistance generally moved in the same direction as, rather than counter to, the business cycle and was not consistent with fiscal or monetary policy.[25] As a consequence, credit assistance loan flows apparently contributed little to economic stabilization or to coordinated economic management efforts.

A good portion of federal financial assistance has been directed toward economic activities characterized by high risk or low earnings, such as housing, agriculture, and troubled industries.[26] Political judgments about profitability, risks, and social benefits and costs are, in these and similar instances, substituted for private market judgments. The economic costs of this substitution are obviously difficult to measure, but cannot be ignored. One key question is whether these costs are taken into account as credit programs are initiated and expanded or are subordinated to the political pressures from beneficiary groups.

The true costs of federal credit activity are not always, or even predominantly, tangible and direct. In addition to explicit interest subsidies, administrative costs, and default liabilities, federal credit programs can change the composition, if not the level, of investment. Since these changes and their effects are diffused and hidden, however, there is an inherent asymmetry between the benefits and costs of federal credit activity.

Fiscal and Political Accountability

The American public is now aware of some serious problems with the federal budget. Despite efforts to strengthen budget control in Congress and the executive branch, spending continues to grow rapidly, and deficits continue to mount. Because of statutory commitments and contractual obligations the government has assumed in the past, three-fourths of federal spending is automatic (or what the budget designates as "relatively uncontrollable under existing law"). Entitlement programs designed to assist individuals currently account for nearly half the federal budget. Interest payments on the federal debt held by the public exceed 10 percent of total outlays and are expected to pass the $100 billion mark during fiscal 1984.

The problems of control associated with the official budget are obviously severe, but they are at least reasonably well understood. There are no secrets about where spending growth has occurred, nor much question about why.

Whether that growth has been beneficial is debatable, and continued conflicts over attempts to restrain spending are inevitable. The central point, however, is that presidential and congressional budgets allow the public at least some opportunity to impose accountability on elected officials.

Federal credit programs, by comparison, are much more elusive, confounding efforts to hold officials accountable. There is a decided lack of information about the scope, growth, and costs of federal credit assistance. Instead of a reasonably coordinated and coherent policy effort, there are numerous and diverse programs divorced from central control. This absence of control makes it more difficult for public officials to resist pressures to extend subsidies and favors to new constituencies. Meanwhile, the general public remains unaware of the fiscal and economic costs of federal credit activities.

Hidden spending is not an isolated phenomenon. Like direct spending, it raises serious questions about the fiscal responsibility of political institutions. And like direct spending, it poses an immediate challenge to the capabilities and will of the president and Congress. In the case of hidden spending, however, the political obstacles are only part of the problem, albeit a major part. There are a number of technical issues that must be resolved in order to rationalize credit decision making. With credit, one is truly dealing with "the politics of confusion." [27]

Chapter 2

Components of Federal Credit Activity

The expansion of federal credit intervention, like the growth of federal spending, reflects changing perceptions of the federal government's social and economic responsibilities. Prior to the 1930s, there was virtually no credit intervention, and federal spending was restricted to a narrow range of public goods functions, such as national defense and public works. Assistance programs for individuals were essentially limited to veterans benefits and other war-related expenditures.

The governing philosophy of public finance mandated low levels of public expenditures, balanced peacetime budgets, and reductions of war-generated public debt. During the 1920s, for example, federal spending actually declined, and a steady string of budget surpluses reduced the World War I debt by almost one-third.[1]

With the Depression and the New Deal, federal budget policy was broadened to cover a wide range of social and economic objectives. The budget became an instrument for managing and stabilizing the economy, providing assistance to individuals, and distributing aid to regions and industries. By 1940 social welfare spending accounted for almost one-fourth of federal spending, while domestic programs in agriculture, community development and housing, and natural resources amounted to nearly half the entire federal budget.[2]

The reversal of traditional assumptions about the nature and purposes of spending budgets provided the opportunity for initiating credit assistance programs on a substantial scale. The beginning of the "credit budget" is usually traced back to 1932, when the Reconstruction Finance Corporation was established to make loans to businesses and financial institutions threatened by the Depression. Shortly thereafter, additional agencies were created to extend federal credit, primarily to support housing and agriculture. Since the end of World War II credit programs have been extended to other sectors of the economy and to new classes of borrowers. The result has been to transform federal credit assistance from a temporary, emergency measure into a permanent policy instrument for promoting certain economic activities and redistributing economic resources.

While there are some obvious parallels in the expansion of federal spending and federal lending, there are also important distinctions. The composition of the spending and credit budgets has moved along different tracks. Attempts by the executive branch and Congress to tighten controls on direct spending have led to increased utilization of credit assistance. Loan guarantees and off-budget direct lending have grown so rapidly that much of the allocation of economic resources by government now occurs in ways that are effectively outside the discipline of the budget process. Further exceptions to the fiscal model of coordinated, coherent national policy are provided by the growth of government-sponsored enterprises and tax-exempt status for private-purpose state and local government bonds. The development of federal credit programs has, in fact, made integrated economic policy more difficult to formulate and to implement.

Spending and Credit Priorities

One of the major functions of the federal budget is to determine priorities between competing functions and programs. An important point of comparison between presidential budgets and congressional budget resolutions each year is the allocation of total spending among the broad functional categories in the budget, such as defense, health, and income security.[3] It is possible to analyze the credit budget in a similar fashion in order to compare spending and credit priorities.

The Spending Budget

The composition of the spending budget has changed markedly over the past several decades, reflecting a clear shift in government priorities. In particular, the relative budget shares allocated to defense and to social welfare programs have been reversed. Defense outlays, which accounted for approximately half of all federal spending during the late 1950s, declined to less than one-fourth in fiscal 1980 (see Table 2.1). "Payments for individuals," which include income transfers and in-kind benefit programs, have moved in the opposite direction and currently account for almost half of the spending budget.

Whether measured as payments for individuals or as the budget functions categorized as "human resources" spending, social welfare expenditures dominate the spending budget. Even under the Reagan administration's budget program, the budget share for human resources spending would decline only marginally by fiscal 1985 (see Table 2.2). What is highly unlikely, however, is any substantial increase in the social welfare allocation, such as the one that occurred during the early 1970s.

Moreover, even if the budget share for defense continues its upward trend

Table 2.1 Budget Shares, Defense versus Payments for Individuals, Fiscal Years 1955–1983

	Percentage of Total Outlays	
Fiscal Year	Defense	Payments for Individuals
1955	58.2	19.0
1960	49.0	24.8
1965	40.1	27.3
1970	40.2	32.3
1975	26.4	46.4
1980	23.6	47.0
1981	24.3	48.2
1982	25.7	47.8
1983 (est.)	26.7	48.7

Source: *Budget of the United States Government, Fiscal Year 1978* (Washington, D.C.: Government Printing Office, 1977), p. 436; *Budget of the United States Government, Fiscal Year 1984* (Washington, D.C.: Government Printing Office, 1983), p. 9-54.

that began in fiscal 1981, the relative priorities accorded defense and social welfare in the spending budget will change only marginally. The most generous defense estimates, as contained in President Reagan's budget program, show defense outlays at over 30 percent of total spending by fiscal 1985. Only a small portion of this, however, represents a direct trade-off with social welfare. By far the greater decrease is projected in the allocations for such functions as agriculture, housing, transportation, and international affairs—the "all other" category shown in Figure 2.1. The budget share allotted for these "general government" spending categories is projected at just over 10 percent in fiscal 1985, or roughly one-half the fiscal 1980 level.

Just as the high levels of spending growth over the past twenty-five years have not been evenly distributed throughout the budget, current efforts to restrain spending likely will not be uniformly applied to all spending programs. In the past, *real* budget growth has been financed through constraints on defense expenditures coupled with a major expansion of total outlays. From 1965 to 1979, for example, federal spending increased by 79 percent in constant dollars. There was, however, practically zero real growth in defense over this period, compared to increases of 240 percent in payments for individuals, 130 percent for interest, and 37 percent for all other expenditures.[4] With real growth in defense now a budget priority—and with another large portion of

Table 2.2 Human Resources Spending, Fiscal Years 1970–1985

Budget Functions[a]	Fiscal Year Outlays (in billions of dollars)						
	1970	1975	1980	1981	1982	1985 (est.)	
Education, employment, training, and social services	$ 7.9	$ 15.9	$ 30.8	$ 31.4	$ 26.3	$ 25.1	
Health (combined)	13.0	25.7	55.2	66.0	74.0	100.5	
Income security (combined)	43.1	108.6	193.1	225.1	248.3	294.6	
Veterans benefits and services	8.7	16.6	21.2	23.0	23.9	26.5	
Total	$72.7	$166.8	$300.3	$345.5	$372.5	$446.7	
Percentage of total budget outlays	37.0%	51.4%	52.1%	52.6%	51.1%	48.6%	

Source: *Budget of the United States Government, Fiscal Year 1978* (Washington, D.C.: Government Printing Office, 1977), pp. 426–30; *Budget of the United States Government, Fiscal Year 1984* (Washington, D.C.: Government Printing Office, 1983), pp. 5-84–5-131, 9-42–9-48.

a. The functions shown for this categorization follow the conventional budget designation.

Figure 2.1 Composition of the Spending Budget, Fiscal Years 1980–1985

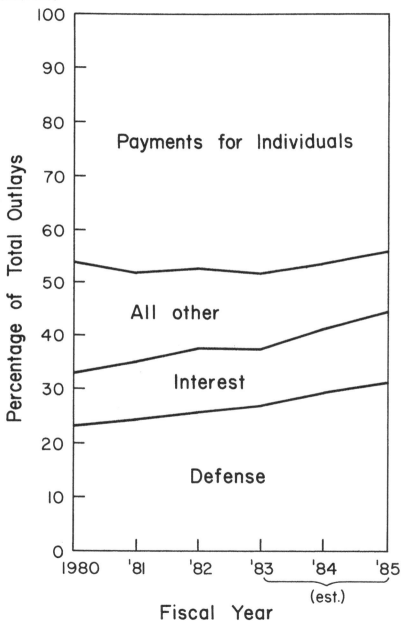

Source: *Budget of the United States Government, Fiscal Year 1984* (Washington, D.C.: Government Printing Office, 1983), p. 9-54.

the budget earmarked for mandatory spending, such as entitlement programs for individuals and interest payments on the federal debt—the target of most budget control proposals is the broad range of programs outside the defense and social welfare areas. While differing in the precise levels of future spending, Reagan administration budgets and congressional budgets reflect a common commitment to reduce spending in a number of areas—agriculture, transportation, energy, and community and regional development. Even if actual reductions are not accomplished, the prospects for increased support in these areas are poor. The priorities in the spending budget, then, are reasonably clear-cut, and the distinctions between competing budget functions are likely to become even sharper in the future.

The Credit Budget

Over the past several decades, federal credit has been concentrated in agriculture and housing programs. Agriculture now accounts for more than two-thirds of new direct lending and about one-sixth of guaranteed lending (see Table 2.3). While housing remains a primary credit assistance area, its "share" of new credit has decreased substantially. In fiscal 1950, for example, housing programs accounted for 97 percent of new guaranteed loan commitments and 57 percent of new direct loan commitments. In fiscal 1982 the corresponding shares for housing were 63 percent for guaranteed loans and 10 percent for direct loans. In addition, loan guarantees for purposes other than housing or agriculture accounted for only 3 percent of new commitments in fiscal 1960; in 1982 they represented more than one-fifth of all new commitments. This growth has been widely distributed among international assistance, energy, education, and transportation programs.

The composition of the credit budget presents a sharp contrast to the direct spending budget. It is dominated not by defense and income security—the two largest functions in the spending budget—but by agriculture and housing. Other functional categories that are well supported in the credit budget are, in many instances, among the smallest in the spending budget. To an extent, these differences merely reflect the fact that credit assistance is more suitable for certain types of programs than for others. It is probable, however, that many credit programs simply could not compete effectively for funding if they were in the form of direct spending. The highly visible and centralized budget process that determines spending tends to respond to the demands of mass constituencies, as in the case of social security and other income security programs, and to national public opinion, as in the case of defense. As a result, the spending budget approximates the fiscal model of coordinated national policy.

Table 2.3 Direct Loan Obligations and Loan Guarantee Commitments, by Function, Fiscal Years 1950–1982

Function	FY 1950	FY 1960	FY 1970	FY 1981	FY 1982
Percentage of New Direct Loan Obligations					
Agriculture	15	19	38	58	69
Housing	57	44	23	16	10
All other	28	37	39	26	21
Total	100	100	100	100	100
Percentage of New Guaranteed Loan Commitments					
Agriculture	0	8	4	15	16
Housing	97	89	82	63	63
All other	3	3	14	22	21
Total	100	100	100	100	100

Source: Figures for 1950–70 are from Congressional Budget Office, *Loan Guarantees: Current Concerns and Alternatives for Control* (Washington, D.C.: Congressional Budget Office, 1979), pp. 32–35, 52–55; the 1981 and 1982 figures (for on-budget agencies) are from *Special Analysis F, Federal Credit Programs, Budget of the United States Government, Fiscal Years 1983–1984.*

The decision-making process for credit programs is considerably less demanding. Control over credit allocations is less centralized. Debates about priorities are virtually nonexistent. The costs of many programs are difficult to estimate, and loan guarantees in particular are often treated as cost-free. These factors make it possible for Congress and the executive branch to expand credit assistance programs, while avoiding difficult and politically unattractive trade-offs with direct spending programs.

The policy priorities of the spending and credit budgets, then, are quite different. Long-term trends in direct spending have narrowed substantially the budget allocation available to support a broad range of domestic and international programs. The expansion of credit programs, however, has provided government decision makers with an alternative means of supporting these programs. When credit and spending are considered together, there is an important modification in the flow of federal assistance (see Figure 2.2). The allocation of resources among competing national needs is thus greatly affected by the growth and proliferation of federal credit programs. As Nancy H. Teeters, a member of the Board of Governors of the Federal Reserve System, pointed out to members of the House Budget Committee, "If direct loans, loan guarantees, and preferential tax treatment were given the same attention

Figure 2.2 Composition of Federal Spending and Federal Lending, Fiscal Year 1982

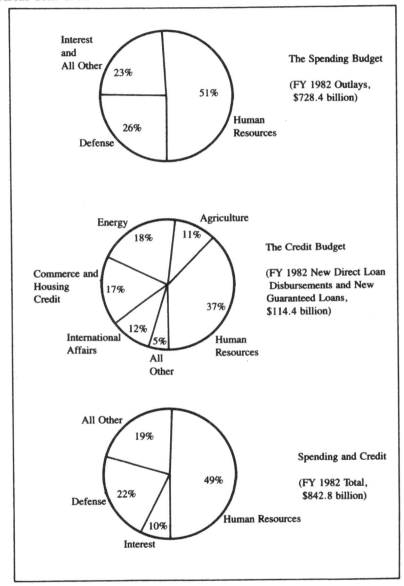

Source: *Budget of the United States Government, Fiscal Year 1984* (Washington, D.C.: Government Printing Office, 1983), pp. 9-42–9-48; *Special Analysis F, Federal Credit Programs, Budget of the United States Government, Fiscal Year 1984* (Washington, D.C.: Government Printing Office, 1983), pp. F-42–F-43.

in the budget process as direct Federal expenditures, the extent of total Federal assistance to particular sectors would look much different from what is currently pictured in the unified budget."[5]

Loan Guarantees

There are two basic types of loan guarantees. In the first, the explicit guarantee, the government acts as a third party in a loan agreement between a borrower and a private lender, pledging to repay principal and interest in the case of default by the borrower. In the second, the government employs long-term contracts, lease agreements, or other financing mechanisms to provide a borrower with funds that can be assigned to pay debt service on a loan. In both instances, the lender's risk is reduced and the borrower's access to credit is enhanced.

The objective of loan guarantees is to channel private credit to particular sectors of the economy and to certain types of borrowers. Federal guarantees encourage lenders to make funds available for designated purposes, such as residential housing or student loans. Borrowers are similarly encouraged, since the federal guarantee usually means lower interest costs. Loan guarantee programs therefore affect both the allocation and the cost of credit, and they are the primary means for advancing federal credit assistance. Since the early 1950s, for example, the volume of loan guarantee commitments has been roughly double that of direct federal lending.[6]

Employed initially for housing and agricultural credit, loan guarantees are now used in a wide variety of policy areas (see Table 2.4). Accompanying this proliferation has been an important qualitative change in the nature of loan guarantee programs. While the largest guarantee programs, especially those in residential housing, are considered to be actuarially sound, much of the recent growth in guarantees has occurred in programs to assist marginal borrowers or to finance large projects and single borrowers. In both cases, the costs and financial risks assumed by government are considerably greater than for traditional loan guarantee programs.

Actuarially Sound Programs

During the Depression the government channeled credit to the housing industry by instituting the Federal Housing Administration (FHA) mortgage guarantee program. Previously, large down-payment requirements and short loan maturities had characterized residential housing credit, and this had greatly

**Table 2.4 Major Loan Guarantee Programs, Fiscal Year 1982
(in billions of dollars)**

Program/Agency	New Commitments	Total Outstanding
International security assistance	3.1	11.7
Farmers Home Administration farm loans	12.3	53.7
Commodity Credit Corporation export credits	1.5	2.6
Rural Electrification Administration	5.6	20.1
Energy research and technology	0.0	2.1
Subsidized low-rent public housing	13.3	20.8
Federal Housing Administration	18.6	142.2
Government National Mortgage Association	36.4	115.5
Federal ship financing fund	0.6	7.2
Veterans Administration housing loans	6.0	108.8
Export-Import Bank	5.8	6.1
Student loans	6.2	22.7
Small Business Administration business loans	2.0	9.9
Tennessee Valley Authority	4.5	1.2

Source: *Special Analysis F, Federal Credit Programs, Budget of the United States Government, Fiscal Year 1984* (Washington, D.C.: Government Printing Office, 1983), pp. F-32–F-39; *Budget of the United States Government, Fiscal Year 1984* (Washington, D.C.: Government Printing Office, 1983), p. 5-93.

restricted the number of borrowers. In order to encourage private lenders to issue long-term, self-amortizing residential mortgages and to accept smaller down payments, the government assumed the risk by insuring that interest and principal would be paid.

The FHA program was designed to be self-financing. Relatively small loans were made to a large number of borrowers, thereby pooling the risks. Operating costs and actuarial estimates of potential losses were the basis for fees and premiums paid by borrowers to obtain government guarantees. Within a few years, the FHA program succeeded in transforming financing arrangements for residential credit. The long-term, fixed-rate mortgage gained widespread acceptance and became a fixture of the housing market even without government guarantees. It has continued to dominate mortgage financing for more than forty years, although the recent surge in interest rates has led to increased use of alternative financing arrangements.

The continuation of government insurance for residential mortgages despite the availability of private mortgage insurance can be attributed to two main factors. First, FHA-insured mortgages require very low down payments (as low as 3 to 5 percent), which serves as a subsidy for borrowers, who would otherwise have to provide substantially higher down payments to qualify for private mortgage insurance. Second, FHA mortgages can be easily sold by mortgage bankers to the Government National Mortgage Association, which repackages them into bonds that also carry a government guarantee. This facilitates the flow of credit to the residential housing market. While the initial objective of federally insured mortgages was achieved relatively quickly, the program has developed such strong support among lenders and borrowers that FHA insurance continues to be a central feature of the residential housing market.

The FHA model has been used as well to finance property improvement loans, to guarantee mortgages for veterans through the Veterans Administration (VA), and to expand credit for farm-operating loans through the Farmers Home Administration (FmHA). For many years, these actuarially sound guarantee programs accounted for all but a small percentage of outstanding loan guarantees. In 1960, for example, the FHA, VA, and FmHA programs had almost $50 billion in outstanding guarantees, more than 90 percent of the total outstanding guarantees for all programs.[7] During the 1970s, however, this percentage dropped substantially, as new and rapidly growing programs were established that departed from the traditional actuarial model.

The success of actuarially sound guarantee programs has had two major effects. First, programs designed to be temporary—as the housing and agriculture guarantee programs during the Depression definitely were—have turned into permanent supports for designated sectors of the economy. Thus, in the housing field the government not only provides FHA and VA guarantees but also engages in very substantial secondary market operations designed to increase the volume of available housing credit. The same is true in agriculture, where the farm credit system provides additional credit to farmers and farm cooperatives. Second, the assumption of federal responsibility that was an explicit part of initial guarantee programs has provided the impetus for extending assistance to other sectors of the economy and to new classes of borrowers.

Marginal Borrowers

Under actuarially sound guarantee programs, the pooling of risks among a large number of borrowers may serve to reduce the interest costs to individual borrowers. Since fees and premiums are charged to cover possible losses and loans are secured by marketable property, the potential financial risk to government is minimal. Whatever subsidy borrowers receive is not an explicit part of the government guarantee. Instead, the guarantee assumes that private credit markets are unable to assess risk accurately; the purpose of the guarantee is to correct that imperfection with a lower but more accurate assessment of risk. For borrowers with appropriate collateral, this adjustment is generally sufficient to insure access to credit.

For other borrowers, however, an explicit subsidy is part of a loan guarantee, either because the government wishes to reduce their interest costs or because there is a greater than normal prospect for default. Guaranteed loans for these marginal borrowers include small business loans, student loans, and housing loans in depressed areas. In each of these, guarantees have been extended despite lack of sufficient collateral, uncertain probability of default, and absence of fees or premiums sufficient for actuarially sound operations. The costs to borrowers are deliberately set below the interest rates they would otherwise pay for credit, assuming they could actually qualify for private credit.

Programs for marginal borrowers are considerably more numerous than actuarially sound programs, although their dollar volume has generally been lower.[8] The gap in outstanding guarantees, however, has narrowed substantially over the past two decades (see Figure 2.3). While outstanding guarantees for actuarially sound programs roughly doubled between 1960 and 1976, the total for programs for marginal borrowers increased from just over $3 billion to nearly $60 billion.

Because of their higher default rates and hidden subsidies, loan guarantees to marginal borrowers often amount to direct grants. The small business loan program administered by the Small Business Administration, for example, has been plagued by high default rates.[9] Default problems have also surfaced in the guaranteed student loan program. The student loan program, in fact, illustrates the unanticipated budgetary consequences that can result from use of the loan guarantee mechanism.

General federal financial support for education is relatively recent. There were scattered federal efforts to aid education, primarily higher education, extending back to the Civil War period, but until the 1950s the emphasis was on grants-in-aid and other forms of direct spending.[10] In 1958 the National Defense Education Act (NDEA) provided federal support for science and

Figure 2.3 Total Guarantees Outstanding for Actuarially Sound Programs and for Programs for Marginal Borrowers

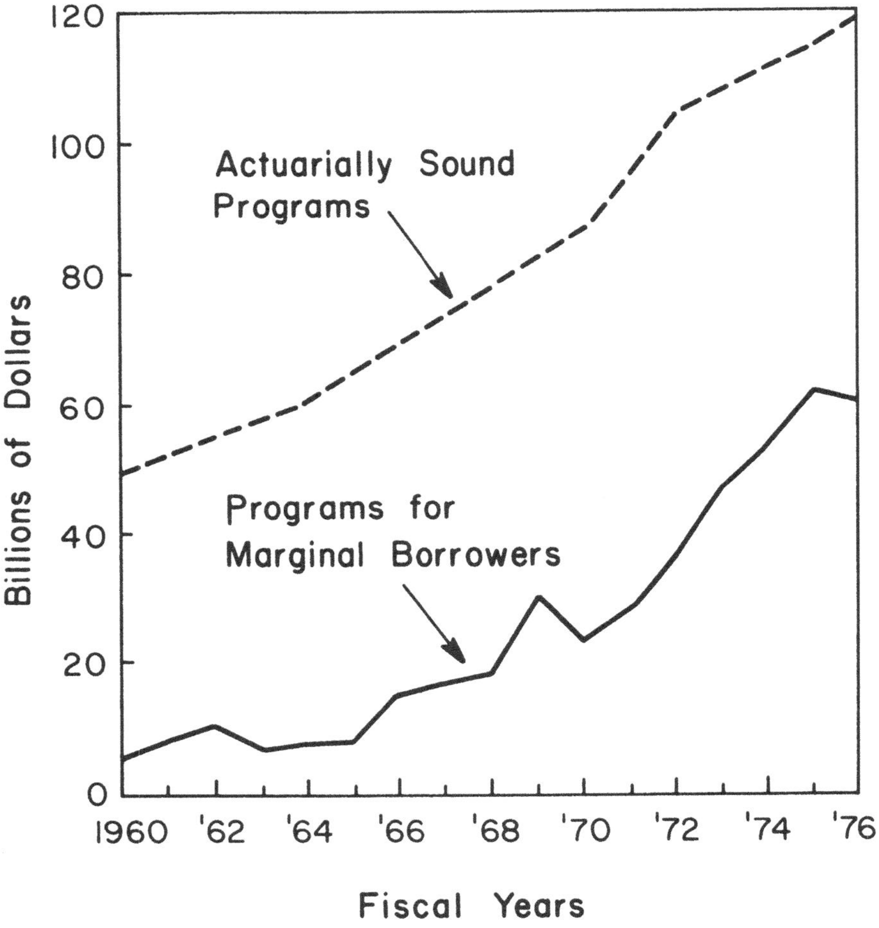

Source: Congressional Research Service, *Federal Loan Guarantees and Their Use as a Mechanism to Correct Market Imperfections, Assist Marginal Borrowers and Finance Discrete Ventures* (Washington, D.C.: Congressional Research Service, 27 April 1977).

mathematics studies at all levels of the educational system and also authorized financial aid, including government loans, for college students. National defense overtones, however, were largely absent when Congress enacted the Elementary and Secondary Education Act of 1965 and the Higher Education Act that same year. Adopted after long periods of controversy, each of these measures endorsed federal responsibility for general education assistance, but they moved along different financial tracks. Support for elementary and secondary education chiefly utilized direct spending, primarily grants-in-aid. Assistance for higher education incorporated credit programs and direct spending.

Part B of Title 5 of the Higher Education Act of 1965 was the genesis of guaranteed, interest-subsidized loans for college students. The Johnson administration, which sponsored the loan guarantee proposal, wanted to provide assistance to a broad segment of the population—including students from middle-income as well as low-income families—at low budgetary cost. By substituting loan guarantees for the direct loan program initiated by the 1958 NDEA legislation, the administration hoped that the amount of credit available for college students could be significantly expanded without any corresponding increase in the budget. Instead, Congress decided to implement loan guarantees and to expand the direct loan program.

From this modest beginning, federal loan programs have become the major element of federal aid to higher education. In 1982 aid to students in the form of direct loans, grants, and subsidized interest payments on guaranteed loans accounted for approximately 90 percent of all general federal outlays for higher education.[11] The guaranteed student loan program differs from most guarantee programs in that there are immediate outlay requirements. Once a student receives a federally guaranteed loan from a private lender—with a 9 percent maximum interest rate—the federal government not only provides a subsidy payment to the lender for the low interest rate but also commits itself to pay full interest on the loan while the student remains in college.[12] This required outlays of $3 billion in fiscal 1982, or almost one-half of all federal outlays for higher education. It is currently estimated that guaranteed student loan outlays will decrease to just over $2 billion by fiscal 1986, but this will still represent more than one-third of higher education outlays.[13]

The guaranteed student loan program functions as an entitlement: the federal government is obligated to provide support for all students meeting statutory eligibility requirements. When Congress liberalized eligibility by removing family income limits in 1978, the impact on participation and borrowing was immediate. Between fiscal years 1977 and 1981 outstanding loan guarantees under the student loan insurance fund rose from $6.2 billion to $22.7 billion; over the same period the level of new commitments increased from less than $2 billion annually to over $6 billion.

There are several types of federal student aid in addition to guaranteed loans. These include student grants (such as the Basic Educational Opportunity, or Pell, grants for needy students), direct loans, and various forms of campus-based aid (such as the college work-study program). The sharpest growth, however, has occurred in the guaranteed student loan program, and it is now threatening to overwhelm other forms of student aid (see Figure 2.4).

Figure 2.4 Federal Aid to Students for Higher Education, Fiscal Years 1971–1983

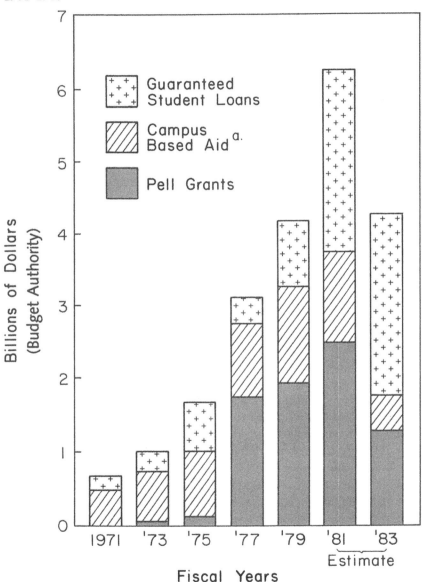

Source: *Budget of the United States Government, Fiscal Year 1983* (Washington, D.C.: Government Printing Office, 1982), p. 5-113.

a. Consists of direct student loans, work study, and other grants from 1971 to 1981.

In 1982 Congress refused to enact major restrictions on the loan guarantee program, but then was required to hold spending in a half-dozen other aid programs at or below fiscal 1981 levels. Of particular interest, Pell grants, which are designed to assist financially disadvantaged students, were cut, while loan guarantees, which are not targeted on low-income groups, were allowed to grow. The chairman of the Senate Budget Committee, Pete Domenici, warned his colleagues that "we must also work to restrain the growth of the guaranteed student loan program, before that program absorbs all the available federal resources for higher education." [14] That warning went unheeded as middle-class students and university administrators launched a massive demonstration and lobbying effort in Congress.[15]

Students receiving guaranteed loans are required to pay an origination fee or premium. These fees are to cover administrative expenses, not to provide a reserve for covering defaults. According to program administrators, the default insurance approach, which was the basis for actuarially sound programs, "was deliberately *not* chosen in order to avoid good student borrowers being penalized for bad risk student borrowers." [16] In effect, program objectives were substituted for fiscal controls, although it was obvious that default costs would have to be financed through general outlays in the absence of adequate reserve funds.

Guaranteed student loans were initiated in order to avoid direct budgetary costs. They have shown, instead, that loan guarantees are far from costless and may have perverse and unintended effects on controllable spending programs. The guaranteed student loan program amounts to a vast subsidy, not just for students but also for the colleges and universities they attend. Whether or not such a subsidy is desirable, the use of the loan guarantee mechanism to finance it has made it much more difficult for Congress and the executive branch to impose coordination and coherence on aid to higher education.

The use of loan guarantees rather than direct grants to extend subsidies to marginal borrowers greatly reduces immediate budgetary costs. It does not, however, eliminate those costs but merely hides or postpones them. The growth of subsidized guarantee programs has been facilitated by the illusion that they are relatively cost-free. Given the record of small business loans, student loans, and programs for other marginal borrowers, that illusion is hard to sustain.

Large Ventures

Over the past decade loan guarantees have also been used to assist large single borrowers and to finance new technological ventures, especially in the field of energy. In 1971, $250 million in federally guaranteed loans was used to re-store the Lockheed Corporation to financial stability. Subsequently, large guarantee programs were authorized to help finance the Amtrak and Conrail systems, to rescue New York City and the Chrysler Corporation from finan-cial collapse, and to fund the synthetic fuels program. These and similar loan guarantees have substantially increased the volume of credit directed toward large borrowers. The total of outstanding guarantees for "discrete ventures," which was negligible through the mid-1960s, climbed to over $3 billion in fiscal 1976.[17] In fiscal 1982 the Chrysler and New York City guarantee pro-grams alone accounted for more than $2.6 billion in outstanding guarantees.[18]

Of course, there is no way to predict whether such a guarantee will succeed in restoring a company's financial stability. The circumstances of each guaran-tee program are reasonably distinct, so that default rates cannot be applied from one program to another. This is especially true as the number of guaran-tees increases. Just one year before the Chrysler program was enacted, $550 million in loan guarantees was authorized for steel industry companies, with very little of the attention or controversy that surrounded the debate over Chrysler. In addition, a variety of loan guarantees have been enacted to stimu-late research and development, new technologies and production, and conser-vation programs in energy, with considerable uncertainty about their potential costs and profitability or the actual liabilities being assumed by the federal government. For guarantees for both large borrowers and new technologies, the perception of low budgetary costs may be illusory, given the default poten-tial. Equally illusory is the perception that costs are associated only with de-fault. As a Senate Budget Committee staff report noted with respect to energy financing guarantee proposals: "In fact, loan guarantees . . . can be costly policy tools. They may reallocate capital, and drive up interest rates in sectors which receive less capital. Some other projects—possibly worthwhile proj-ects—may be unable to secure financing. They thus have an overall impact on the economy that should not be ignored."[19]

The development of federal loan guarantees, then, shows a clear trend away from relatively low-cost, low-risk programs toward much more problematical financing schemes. It is also quite apparent that loan guarantees have been used to extend subsidies to borrowers who would fare considerably less well if forced to compete for direct spending support. In 1980, for example, almost 40 percent of dependent freshmen borrowers under the guaranteed student loan program came from families with incomes above $30,000.[20] Similarly, guarantees for discrete ventures necessarily go to large, corporate borrowers. What may be politically unacceptable as direct spending becomes not only acceptable but quite attractive when loan guarantees are involved.

Direct Lending

Like loan guarantees, direct federal loans are used for a wide variety of purposes. The largest single component is agricultural credit, with existing programs providing federal assistance for rural development and housing, farm operation, crop loans, and rural electrification. In addition, direct loans are used to support low-rent public housing, foreign military and commercial sales, and small businesses (see Table 2.5).

A number of direct loan programs can be traced back to the Depression.[21] Several agencies were created during the New Deal to provide direct credit assistance to support housing and agriculture. For the latter, direct loan programs were instituted to aid small farmers, as well as to fund rural development projects. The Farm Security Administration, for example, was a New Deal "action-agency," authorized to provide low-interest loans to farmers unable to obtain private credit for the purchase and operation of small farms. It was also allowed to furnish direct loans to finance small water-development projects.

The Farm Security Administration was reorganized into the Farmers Home Administration (FmHA) in 1946, and the FmHA was subsequently given increasingly broader authorizations for rural housing credit, emergency farm loans, and watershed development. Through these and other program expan-

**Table 2.5 Major Direct Loan Programs, Fiscal Year 1982
(in billions of dollars)**

Program/Agency	New Obligations	Total Outstanding
International security and development assistance (economic and military)	1.8	17.9
Agricultural credit (general)*	4.2	0.8
Rural housing and development*	4.0	0.6
Crop loans and export credits	12.3	20.8
Housing and Urban Development	4.0	13.2
Export-Import Bank	3.5	16.6
Small Business Administration	0.9	9.2
Rural electrification/telephone bank	1.3	10.9

Source: *Special Analysis F, Federal Credit Programs, Budget of the United States Government, Fiscal Year 1984* (Washington, D.C.: Government Printing Office, 1983), pp. F-14–F-20.
   a. Does not include repurchases of loan assets.

sions the FmHA became one of the largest sources of federal credit, extending both direct loans and loan guarantees. During the 1950s, new commitments for FmHA direct loans averaged less than $230 million annually. This more than doubled over the next decade, and during the 1970s the volume of annual credit rose to an average of over $4.7 billion.[22]

The Rural Electrification Administration (REA), also established under the New Deal, was authorized to furnish low-interest direct loans for the construction of electrical facilities in rural areas. In 1949 a companion program was enacted for rural telephone facilities. REA programs have been extremely popular in farm constituencies because of their very low interest rates and long loan maturities. REA-assisted electrical cooperatives now operate in forty-six states and cover 75 percent of the land mass, but only 10 percent of the electrical consumers, in the nation.[23] The political potency of this network has been impressive. In 1973 Congress moved the REA off budget in order to protect it from spending ceilings and impoundments being imposed by the Nixon administration.[24] The protection was sufficient to allow new direct lending by the REA to increase from less than $520 million in fiscal 1973 to nearly $1.4 billion in fiscal 1980.[25] Congressional solicitousness toward the REA surfaced again in 1981. Contending that rural areas no longer required subsidized loans, the Reagan administration sought to curb REA loan programs, but Congress rejected the proposed cuts after a major lobbying campaign organized by the National Rural Electric Cooperative Association.[26]

A third agricultural lending program is administered by the Commodity Credit Corporation (CCC); this agency, which was made part of the Department of Agriculture in 1939, was given primary responsibility for loan programs to carry out price-support and related policies. The CCC was allowed to borrow directly from the Treasury in order to supplement its initial capitalization. The CCC's loan programs for price supports and exports are currently exempt from appropriations control, and its net outlays are highly variable. Actual credit transactions are substantial, with new commitments averaging approximately $7 billion annually during fiscal years 1979–81. Moreover, CCC loans are nonrecourse transactions. The CCC makes loans to farmers based upon the support prices for crops used as collateral. If market prices fall below support levels, farmers can repay the CCC with crops instead of cash even though the collateral value is below the loan amount.

The use of government credit to finance exports is not limited to agriculture. The Export-Import Bank has for many years furnished direct loans as well as loan guarantees to foreign governments to facilitate the sale of non-agricultural products. In fiscal 1982 the bank had over $16 billion in outstanding direct loans, and new obligations for fiscal years 1979–81 averaged nearly

$5 billion annually. In recent years the bank's direct loans and loan guarantees have been heavily concentrated in commercial aircraft, nuclear power, and high-technology export sales. Approximately two-thirds of the bank's lending activity in 1981, for example, directly benefited seven large commercial exporters, primarily·the Boeing and Westinghouse corporations.[27]

Direct loans are also issued to foreign governments to underwrite various development projects, to provide economic assistance, and to finance purchases of military weapons from the United States. Economic development loans were first employed on a substantial scale after World War II to assist Britain and other western European governments in postwar recovery. Their use was revived during the late 1960s to assist underdeveloped nations, and by the end of fiscal 1981 outstanding direct loans under the economic support fund and international development assistance exceeded $16 billion.

Off-budget financing greatly reduces the visible budget outlays required to support direct lending. Of the nearly $56 billion in new direct loans issued during fiscal 1981, only $5 billion surfaced as outlays for on-budget agencies, compared to $21 billion for off-budget agencies. (The remaining $30 billion was accounted for by repayments and other adjustments of previous loans.) This goes a long way toward explaining why Congress has repeatedly rejected proposals from the executive branch and its own budget committees that off-budget spending be incorporated into the budget. The off-budget option provides protection for direct lending programs that might otherwise have great difficulty in competing for spending dollars.

Extra-Budget Credit

Direct lending and loan guarantees by federal agencies (whether on-budget or off-budget) are not the only types of federal credit activity. A complete picture of federal credit policy necessarily includes the roles played by government-sponsored enterprises and tax-exempt credit. The effect of both is to enlarge significantly the degree of federal involvement in credit markets, although each presents very different problems for attempts at budget control.

Government-Sponsored Enterprises

Several organizations have been established and chartered by the federal government to perform specialized credit functions, in particular to act as financial intermediaries serving designated sectors of the economy. These include the Federal National Mortgage Association (FNMA), the Federal Home Loan

Bank System, the Farm Credit Administration, and the Student Loan Marketing Association (SLMA). Each of these is now privately owned, although all but the SLMA were at one time either partially or fully owned by the federal government.

Despite private ownership, there are links between government-sponsored enterprises and the federal government that distinguish them from other private lending institutions. Government-sponsored enterprises are subject to federal supervision, coordinate their operations with the Treasury Department, and carry out federally designed programs. This association carries with it tax exemptions and other preferences and allows government-sponsored enterprises to offer their securities as investments of federally regulated institutions. The widespread assumption that the federal government ultimately backs these organizations, despite the absence of formal guarantees, means that they are able to borrow funds in private credit markets at rates very close to those paid by the government. The FNMA, for example, is authorized to borrow up to $2.25 billion directly from the Treasury Department if it should encounter financial difficulties. This helps to explain why the FNMA is usually able to borrow funds at less than half a percentage point higher than the Treasury on one-year notes and why other government-sponsored enterprises enjoy similarly favorable rates.

The purpose served by government-sponsored enterprises is to expand the credit available for specified activities—housing, agriculture, and student loans. They accomplish this by borrowing and then using funds either to lend directly or to buy loans already made by private lenders. Initially, the financing provided by government-sponsored enterprises was chiefly aimed at stabilizing available credit, lending under tight monetary conditions and being repaid as monetary conditions eased. For the past several years, however, the emphasis has been on expansion rather than stabilization of credit for designated activities.

The FNMA and the Federal Home Loan Bank System, for example, deal with housing credit. The FNMA, which was created to establish a secondary market in residential mortgages, purchases mortgages held by private lenders and funds these purchases through mortgage-backed securities that it offers in private credit markets. Mortgage bankers have additional funds for new mortgages, while private investors have a very low-risk (perhaps risk-free) investment. So long as the earning power of the FNMA's mortgage portfolio (which stood at just under $60 billion at the end of fiscal 1981) exceeds its borrowing costs, it can turn a profit, while providing additional liquidity for the mortgage bankers it serves. The federal home loan banks operate in a different fashion, advancing or lending funds directly to savings and loan associations; the Federal Home Loan Mortgage Corporation (FHLMC), an affiliated organization, buys mortgages like the FNMA, although it has been shifting its portfolio toward conventional mortgages insured by private insurers, leaving the FNMA as the primary holder of FHA- and VA-insured mortgages. Outstanding loans by the federal home loan banks and FHLMC exceeded $90 billion at the end of fiscal 1981 and are expected to total $145 billion by the end of fiscal 1983.

The Farm Credit Administration includes three banking systems—intermediate credit banks, land banks, and banks for cooperatives, all of which are organized on a regional basis. The farm credit system was established under the 1916 Federal Farm Loan Act and enlarged under the 1933 Farm Credit Act. In 1968 the credit and cooperative banks became wholly privately owned by repaying their federal equity capital. The federal land banks had earlier moved from government to private ownership.

The components of the farm credit system serve different purposes. The federal land banks provide long-term mortgage loans to farmers. The intermediate banks supply credit for farm production and improvements. The banks for cooperatives lend to cooperatives of farmer borrowers. Taken together, the farm credit system accounts for a large portion of total agricultural credit—38 percent of long-term farm mortgage debt and 25 percent of short-term debt in 1980.[28] The outstanding loans under the Farm Credit Administration exceeded $75 billion at the end of fiscal 1981 and are estimated at $100 billion for fiscal 1983.

The SLMA was created to support the guaranteed student loan program. In the past, it has purchased student loans from private lenders, while borrowing directly from the Federal Financing Bank (FFB). In 1983 the SLMA was scheduled to switch from FFB borrowing to private credit markets. The SLMA is the smallest of the government-sponsored enterprises, with outstanding loans of $6.0 billion in fiscal 1982. Its growth, however, has been quite rapid—from $81 million in net credit advanced in fiscal 1975 to $1.7 billion in fiscal 1982.

Since the mid-1970s, lending by government-sponsored enterprises has grown very rapidly. The amount of outstanding credit, in the form of direct loans and loan guarantees advanced by government-sponsored enterprises, is estimated at over $285 billion for fiscal 1983, a four-fold increase over the total in fiscal 1975. In fiscal 1975 net credit advanced (new loans minus repayments) amounted to $5.6 billion, compared to $43.3 billion for fiscal 1982. Of all credit advanced under federal auspices, the percentage accounted for by government-sponsored enterprises has grown from approximately 20 percent to well over 40 percent over this same period.

While government-sponsored enterprises have a major impact on credit allocation in the economy, they are not a formal part of the government's credit budget. Their private ownership provides them with a degree of legal protection from executive and congressional efforts to control credit programs, and this is supplemented by the political support of the constituencies that they serve. As a result, they continue to operate in relative obscurity. "For all practical purposes," concluded a recent study, "application of federal influence through government sponsored enterprises lies outside effective federal policy oversight." [29]

Tax-Exempt Bonds

Interest on state and local government obligations has been exempt from federal income tax since 1913. For several decades this exemption was used almost exclusively to support state and local government borrowing for public purposes, such as construction of government buildings and facilities. Beginning in the 1960s, however, it was utilized with increasing frequency to support private uses and is currently available for such purposes as industrial development, industrial pollution control, private nonprofit hospital construction, housing, and student loans. State and local governments can, in effect, transfer their own tax privileges to these private activities. Since the interest on their bonds is exempt from federal taxation, the interest rates are generally much lower than those for comparable private securities. The private borrowers who are able to take advantage of this financing option thus enjoy an interest subsidy from the federal government.

Since the mid-1970s most of the growth in the financing of tax-exempt bonds has been accounted for by private purpose credit. Of the $35 billion in new bonds in 1976, about three-fourths was for state and local government public purpose use. In 1982 nearly half of the more than $87 billion in new financing was for private purpose bonds, and this share is projected at the same level in 1983. [30]

A large component of private purpose tax-exempt financing is for industrial development bonds, which are currently available in all but three states. [31] From 1976 to 1981 industrial development bond issues increased from $1.4 billion to $10.5 billion, or approximately 40 percent of all private purpose tax-exempt financing. In a majority of states offering industrial development bonds, there are no meaningful restrictions on the projects eligible for support. [32] As a result, many large and profitable private enterprises are able to take advantage of the interest rate differentials that accompany tax-exempt bonds. [33]

The interest subsidies involved are impressive. The estimated present value of the private-use tax loss on new bond issues was just under $10 billion in 1981 and is estimated at over $15 billion for 1983.[34] This loss in federal revenue translates into interest rate subsidies for private borrowers. It does not, of course, affect spending totals in the federal budget, but the return to borrowers is the same as a direct grant from the federal government.

While tax-exempt financing affects the cost and allocation of credit in a manner similar to other forms of federal credit assistance, control can be achieved only through statutory changes in the tax code. Action was taken to curb private purpose financing for housing under the Reconciliation Act of 1980 and to restrict the use of industrial development bonds as part of the 1982 tax bill, but the long-term effects of these efforts are uncertain. Housing bonds, for example, are expected to increase substantially in fiscal 1983 and to decline thereafter. Small-issue industrial development bonds are expected to decrease slightly in fiscal 1983 but subsequently to grow rapidly.[35]

Tax-exempt financing for private purposes is a clear example of explicit federal subsidization, but there is considerable controversy over just what benefits are achieved other than the obvious advantage realized by private purpose borrowers. Neither the federal government nor most state governments have made any serious attempt to define the appropriate and desirable uses of this form of credit allocation and to insure that tax-exempt financing conforms to this definition. Ironically, the major impetus to restrict private purpose bonds comes not from any comprehensive analysis of credit policy but rather from the pressure on Congress and the executive branch to raise additional revenues in order to narrow budget deficits.

There are other forms of tax preference that affect credit allocations, such as investment tax credits and personal deductions for mortgage interest on residential housing. Tax-exempt credit, however, is generally considered to be among the most visible and direct forms of tax preference influencing credit allocations. And it provides a sharp illustration of the piecemeal fashion in which federal credit policy has developed.

Credit Programs and Credit Policy

The growth of federal credit programs suggests the absence of coordinated and comprehensive credit policy. Programs of a bewildering variety and complexity have been instituted on a piecemeal basis with relatively little attention by Congress and the executive branch to their cumulative impact on credit or their real costs. Federal housing insurance, initially instituted to correct market imperfections, has been maintained and expanded long after these imperfections were corrected. Additional guarantee programs have been established to assist marginal borrowers with federal subsidies and, at the same time, to avoid accurate accounting of costs in federal budgets. Costs have also been hidden through off-budget financing of direct loan programs.

The evidence is reasonably clear that the impetus for much of the growth in federal credit assistance stems from the illusion that it is costless, rather than from considered judgments about the relative programmatic merits of credit aid versus spending aid. The absence of effective fiscal controls on credit programs has, in fact, made credit aid a politically attractive alternative to direct spending. And the absence of these controls reflects a long-term uncertainty about the appropriate procedures for coordinating spending and credit.

Chapter 3

Accounting for Federal Credit

A precondition for effective budget control is consistent and accurate accounting. This precondition is generally satisfied by the current treatment of direct spending programs. Appropriate handling of the various types of credit programs, however, has proved to be much more elusive. There remain important disagreements between executive branch officials, members of Congress, and agency personnel over basic accounting issues that determine the budgetary treatment of certain very large credit programs. According to the General Accounting Office, the resulting anomalies and inconsistencies prevent credit assistance activities from being "appropriately reflected in the budget."[1] In comparison to other policy tools, "credit assistance is probably the least well understood in its workings, is the most difficult to assess from a cost effectiveness perspective, and has perhaps the greatest potential of being misused."[2]

Accounting procedures used for credit programs are not simply technical issues; they have important policy implications. The amount and quality of information available for specific programs, as well as their relative visibility, are a function of budgetary treatment. Measurements of costs, comparisons with alternative policy tools, and judgments about macroeconomic effects are also affected by these procedures. When critics charge that "largely because of the misleading and incomplete accounting of federal credit programs in budget documents, credit has long appeared a virtually costless form of government intervention," they are voicing important concerns.[3] First, it is possible that credit programs will be used instead of direct spending or other policy tools, regardless of program considerations, because costs are partially or completely hidden. Second, differential treatment of budget costs between various credit programs may encourage the use of relatively less visible types of assistance, again subordinating program considerations.

For more than two decades the executive branch and Congress have wrestled with the programmatic and budget-control implications of incomplete and inconsistent accounting. Progress, however, has been painfully slow. Major weaknesses remain in the procedures governing sales of loan assets by lending agencies and the utilization of guaranteed loans. These weaknesses have become much more serious since the advent of the Federal Financing Bank in

1973. Created to centralize and coordinate agency borrowing, the bank has had the unintended effect of encouraging the use of questionable accounting practices and exacerbating budget-control problems.

Credit Transactions in the Budget

At one level the accounting problems associated with credit programs involve basic distinctions between spending and lending. For spending, the outlays required to implement a given program provide a reasonably comprehensive assessment of costs. In addition, the outlays are "exhaustive," for "once the money is disbursed by the government, none of it is recovered."[4]

For credit programs, no single measurement serves the same purpose. The gross flow of credit extended in the form of new loans during a fiscal year, for example, represents the volume of credit activity. Unlike direct spending, however, loans are not exhaustive. The government lends the funds in exchange for the borrower's promise of repayment. Repayments of previous loans, or the expiration of prior loan guarantees, must therefore be taken into account. The net flow of resources—new credit being extended minus old credit being repaid or recalled—is the appropriate indication of the change in an agency's financial position during the year. Neither gross nor net flows, however, necessarily measure costs, since these depend on the specific characteristics of a loan program, such as the interest charged, the likelihood of loss or default, and administrative expenses. In sum, the costs of a credit program are not the same as program activity.

A second level of difficulty derives from accounting procedures used for credit program transactions.[5] Most credit agencies are authorized to borrow, either from the public or the Treasury, in order to help finance their programs. This borrowing is treated as a means of financing. Borrowing and subsequent repayments by an agency affect its fund balance and liabilities, but neither transaction is recorded in the agency's outlays or expenditures.

When an agency lends funds, the transaction is considered program activity, and the loan principal is recorded as an outlay. Subsequent repayments of the loan by the borrower to the agency are then treated as offsetting receipts or negative outlays. If a loan is fully repaid, its final budgetary cost is zero; the positive and negative outlays will balance out, although not usually in the same fiscal year.

This is reasonably straightforward, but there are, inevitably, complications. In addition to direct appropriations from Congress and borrowing through the issuance of bonds or notes, credit agencies can finance their operations through the sale of loans from their existing portfolios. The important distinction is that sales of prior loans, or loan assets, are treated for budgetary purposes as offsetting receipts or negative outlays, as would be the case if the borrower paid back the loan. An agency that is able to sell its prior loans for an amount equivalent to new loans during a fiscal year has no budget outlays.

From an agency standpoint, the budgetary incentive to sell previous loans is obvious. As an additional benefit, the agency is able to replenish its capital to make new loans without additional appropriations or borrowing. The budgetary loophole associated with this practice emerges when the loans are not actually sold.

The relatively small size, comparatively low interest, and uncertain risk that characterize individual loans in a broad variety of federal credit programs do not make them attractive opportunities for private investors. Unable to market individual loans, a number of agencies have sold not the actual loans but rather shares in large pools of loans. Whether these types of sales are, in fact, legitimate sales of loan assets or simply another form of agency borrowing has been hotly debated for more than two decades. The issue is significant. If the billions of dollars now being treated as loan asset sales each year are instead treated as agency borrowing—because the criteria for actual transfers of assets are not satisfied—the immediate effect is to increase the size of the affected agencies' budgets by that amount, with a corresponding increase in unified budget outlays and deficit.

Like alternative financing methods, alternative ways of lending can have budgetary implications for the agency involved. A direct loan results in budget outlays. A loan guarantee, however, is not considered to be a budgetary transaction, and the agency issuing the guarantee does not record any outlays. On an agency's budget, loan guarantees are cost-free in comparison to direct loans.

The budgetary treatment of loan guarantees becomes misleading, however, when the borrower holding the guarantee sells it in the government securities market. Borrowers with 100 percent federal guarantees can convert their guarantees into direct loans, the financing for which comes not through the originating agency's budget—as would be the case with a direct loan issued by the agency—but rather through Treasury borrowing. Since 1974 the Federal Financing Bank has routinized such conversions and, not incidentally, encouraged the use of loan guarantees.

These seemingly technical issues have been the subject of long-standing disputes. Presidential budget commissions have emphasized consistency and accuracy in the budgetary treatment of credit activities. Lending agencies have been concerned with the programmatic effects of different forms of budgetary treatment. Presidents and members of Congress have tried to balance both sets of concerns, usually with little success. The resulting lack of control over credit activities that benefit from inconsistent or anomalous budgetary treatment, however, has revived the effort to integrate credit programs and the budget more effectively.

Developing Controversies

Prior to initiation of the unified budget format in 1968, several different budgets were used to present federal outlay and revenue data. The administrative budget, which usually received the greatest public attention, showed expenditures and receipts of general funds but excluded the financial transactions of the large and growing trust funds.[6] The consolidated cash budget, which was presented concurrently, was the most comprehensive, incorporating trust fund and general fund transactions as well as net lending expenditures. The national income accounts budget was similar to the consolidated cash format but did not record loan activity and utilized a different method for dealing with new expenditure obligations.

The unified budget, which remains the basic statement of federal finances, includes general funds and trust funds, along with expenditures for net lending (new direct loans minus repayments). The computation of total new authority to obligate funds includes both spending and lending authority. Use of a simple, comprehensive budget was the major recommendation of the President's Commission on Budget Concepts, which had been appointed by President Johnson in 1967. While the commission's major emphasis was on a budget format for direct spending, it gave considerable attention to the proper integration of spending and lending. The commission's report stated that "one of the most difficult questions . . . is how Federal loan outlays should be reflected appropriately in the budget."[7] Included in a number of proposals as to how this might be accomplished were requirements for measuring the subsidy elements in loan programs, distinguishing between legitimate loans and grants or transfers disguised as loans, and separating lending from spending in analyzing the budget's impact on income and employment.

Two problem areas received special attention. The first was the budgetary treatment of various forms of loan sales by federal agencies. The second was the proliferation of loan guarantee and insurance programs. In both cases, the commission expressed concern that major budgetary evasions might be developing.

Loan Asset Sales

The term *loan asset sale* describes a refinancing, or rollover, procedure in which agencies acquire new capital to make loans by selling prior loans. Since federal agencies are not investors, their basic function has been performed once loans have been made for designated public purposes. If these loans can then be sold to outside groups, capital is generated to support additional loans. As financial intermediaries rather than investors, agencies are less interested in future repayments than in immediate cash to refinance their loan portfolios.

When a government loan is made, a loan asset is created, in the form of a note or other debt instrument obligating the borrower to repay. This asset or promise of repayment can then be sold. When a loan asset is sold outright to a private investor, there is no question about the proper budgetary treatment. Since private financing has been substituted for agency financing, the transaction is an offset against new lending.

Questions are raised, however, when the generally accepted criteria for an outright sale are not satisfied. These criteria include actual transfer of the loan asset to the buyer, along with the responsibility for servicing the loan and assuming the risk. For many government credit programs, sales of individual loans under these conditions are impractical. Risk may be too high, or interest return too low, or servicing costs disproportionate to the size of the loan. As an alternative, a number of agencies have, over the years, created pools of individual loans and then sold shares in these pools to investors. The marketability of these pool sales has usually required various "sweeteners"—agency guarantees of payment, higher interest rates than the underlying loans in the pool, and assumption by the agency of any losses on loans in the pool. For purchasers of shares in pool sales, there is usually no risk, no responsibility for servicing individual loans, and no direct ownership of the loan assets included in the pool.

Several types of instruments have been used to carry out this pooling procedure—certificates of participation, certificates of beneficial interest, and, most recent, certificates of beneficial ownership. The distinctions between these are relatively minor. More important is that each provides the means for raising funds without selling individual loans, and each has been attacked as a disguised form of borrowing.

Sales of shares in loan pools were initiated during the 1930s by the Commodity Credit Corporation, which used participation certificates to finance its commodity loans. Participation certificates were used as well during the liquidation of the Reconstruction Finance Corporation in 1954 and, during the early 1960s, by the Export-Import Bank, Federal National Mortgage Association, and Veterans Administration.

In 1962, President Kennedy's Committee on Federal Credit Programs strongly endorsed loan asset sales as fulfilling the objective of substituting private for public credit and also being an "appropriate source of funds for new loans."[8] The committee was less enthusiastic, however, about the use of participation certificates as opposed to direct loan asset sales. Participation certificates, it was stated, should be confined to exceptional, high-risk cases, and even then only as an interim financing procedure.[9]

Despite this caveat, lending agencies continued to push to receive authorization for participation certificate sales, and the Johnson administration sponsored legislation promoting the use of participation certificates to refinance more than $30 billion in outstanding federal loans. As approved by Congress, the Participation Sales Act of 1966 was narrower than the original Johnson bill. It authorized only six agencies to use participation certificates, required that certificate sales be coordinated through the Federal National Mortgage Association, and made certificate sales subject to annual limits in appropriations bills. First-year sales were limited to $3.2 billion, but it was estimated that loan assets of approximately $11 billion would subsequently be sold through participation certificates.

There was considerable opposition to the participation sales legislation. Opponents charged that participation certificates were nothing more than a gimmick designed to hide new spending, keep down the deficit, and evade the public debt limit.[10] The focus of the debate was whether participation certificates were actual loan asset sales or simply another form of borrowing. Minority views contained in the House Banking Committee's report on the participation sales act noted that under a legitimate loan sale "title passes, the purchaser acquires possession, the purchaser assumes the burdens of servicing the loan and . . . any risk of default."[11] By contrast, in a participation sale the agency "pooling the loans retains possession of the assets, . . . continues to [service] the loans, [and] remains exposed to the risk of default."[12] According to private critics of participation sales, "What is being sold . . . is in reality the credit of the United States."[13] And while "presumably no one would seriously contend that a loan extended by a Federal credit agency to . . . a small business involved private credit if the funds had originated with the sale of a Treasury bond to a private investor," there was no difference at all if "the funds employed originate with the sale of PC's."[14] The financing was through borrowing, not loan asset sales.

During deliberations of the President's Commission on Budget Concepts the following year, members representing the Johnson administration defended participation certificate sales against these charges, countering that the sales did not "call upon the revenues or general borrowing of the Treasury," and it was this call that the "net lending figure [in the budget] should equal." [15] A majority of the commission, however, rejected this position. The final report issued by the commission stated the "firm" conviction that "participation certificates, regardless of their advantages or disadvantages on other scores, represent a means of financing the budget rather than an offset to expenditures in determining the amount of the deficit to be financed." [16] The commission thus implicitly endorsed the view presented in an accompanying staff paper that "treatment of the now sizable PC sales as a reduction in budget expenditures and budget deficit has perhaps done more to undermine public and congressional confidence in the integrity of budget totals than any other single issue." [17]

The Johnson administration finally bowed to this criticism. In the president's fiscal 1969 budget, more than $3 billion was added to expenditure totals (in a budget well under $200 billion) simply by not treating participation certificate sales as offsetting expenditures. The immediate pain was eased somewhat since the new unified budget format was introduced at the same time. With almost $40 billion in additional spending resulting from a change in budget format, the loss of participation sales offsets was relatively tolerable.

Within a short time, however, lending agencies were searching for ways to circumvent the new budget rules. The Export-Import Bank was the first to take action, initiating sales of certificates of beneficial interest. The bank maintained these were legitimate loan asset sales, an interpretation challenged by, among others, the General Accounting Office (GAO). For the GAO, certificates of beneficial interest were yet another way to borrow funds, while inappropriately offsetting outlays. The dispute was finally resolved in 1971, when the bank was given off-budget status. In an unusual defense, the House Banking Committee noted that off-budget status would eliminate the need to use certificate sales to keep net budget outlays low, since the bank's outlays would no longer be "calculated in the overall Federal budget." [18]

Other agencies also discontinued the use of participation certificates when these no longer counted as offsets to outlays and turned to other forms of asset sales. The FmHA and REA were especially active in attempting to gain relief from the stricter accounting procedures. When block sales of loans proved to be impractical, the FmHA and REA persuaded the Nixon administration to propose the use of certificates of beneficial ownership as sales of loan assets to offset budget outlays. This authorization was included in Title 2 of the agriculture appropriations act of 1975. The statutory language empowered the secretary of agriculture to sell certificates of beneficial ownership to the Treasury or to private investors and to treat these sales as sales of loan assets "notwithstanding the fact that the Secretary . . . holds the debt instruments evidencing the loans and holds or reinvests payments thereon." [19]

For the FmHA and REA, the certificate of beneficial ownership (CBO) was a unique opportunity to offset new loans and keep budget outlays down. Agency use of this device was protected by statute and therefore could not be reversed by budget officials in the executive branch. In addition, authorization for the use of CBOs coincided with creation of the Federal Financing Bank, which soon became the almost exclusive buyer for a growing volume of CBOs.

Loan Guarantees

The budgetary treatment of loan asset sales was a continuing problem during the 1960s, but at least there was a clear-cut—if temporary—solution available. More difficult was the issue of how to handle loan guarantees. The Commission on Budget Concepts, for example, recognized that stricter accounting for direct loan programs might lead to "further expansion of guaranteed and insured loans not warranted by program considerations." [20] Despite its concern, the commission was unable to agree on specific recommendations for handling loan guarantees, registering instead its support for "coordinated surveillance and direction of all Federal lending activity—direct and guaranteed." [21]

The issue of loan guarantees and budget control was taken up again as part of Congress's budget reform deliberations in 1973 and 1974. Initial proposals called for treating guaranteed lending as budget authority. This would have made loan guarantees subject to the targets and ceilings contained in concurrent budget resolutions and to controls on backdoor spending, as well as to the general discipline of the budget process. [22]

The final version of the 1974 Congressional Budget and Impoundment Control Act, however, specifically excluded loan guarantees from the definition of budget authority. [23] The exclusion was explained in the report issued by the Senate Rules and Administration Committee, which amended the original budget reform bill: "Such [insured and guaranteed] loans are not direct obligations of the United States, and a liability is incurred only in the case of default. Thus, it would not be appropriate to regard such contingent liabilities as budget authority for purposes of determining the appropriate levels in the budget resolution. Nor should loan guarantees be subjected to the new procedures for handling backdoor spending authority." [24]

This was a clear-cut victory for congressional committees that had jurisdiction over loan guarantee programs and were fearful that such programs might not fare well if they were subject to a comprehensive budget process. During final House debate, Representative Charles Vanik (D-Ohio), a strong supporter of the budget reform legislation, strongly criticized the exclusion of guarantee programs:

> We know that dozens of agencies are avoiding budget control by guaranteeing and insuring loans. We know that major Government agencies have been able to defy the will of Congress because they are excluded from the budget and from budget considerations. We know that these guarantees and insurances, these Government corporations, do provide enormous public interest subsidies and contribute to inflation, all without adequate congressional safeguards or review.[25]

Whether the new congressional budget process could have effectively controlled loan guarantees is, of course, problematic. The absence of any formal controls, however, insured that guaranteed credit would remain relatively invisible and that the indirect costs of such credit would receive only sporadic attention. In addition, just as the newly established Federal Financing Bank added a further dimension to the loan asset sales problem, it had an immediate and significant impact on loan guarantees. Thus, in the period 1973–74 legislative decisions regarding the budgetary treatment of loan asset sales and loan guarantees, along with the creation of the Federal Financing Bank, altered the course of federal credit policy.

The Federal Financing Bank

On 19 December 1973, Congress created the Federal Financing Bank (FFB) as a wholly owned government corporation within the Department of the Treasury "to provide for coordinated and more efficient financing of Federal and federally assisted borrowings from the public."[26] The FFB is, by law, designated as an off-budget agency; its budget authority and outlays are thereby excluded from the unified budget totals. Its management consists of a five-member board of directors, including the secretary of the Treasury as chairman and four additional officers appointed by the president from among executive branch officials. The FFB uses Treasury Department facilities and staff to conduct its operations.

While the FFB was established as a debt-management tool, in which capacity it has functioned with considerable success, an important long-term effect of its operations has been to complicate the budgetary treatment of credit pro-

grams. As a result of strict limitations on the discretionary authority of the
FFB in dealing with other federal agencies, the practically unlimited availability of funds to support its activities, and the inconsistent accounting that
characterizes agency dealings with the FFB, the bank's levels and types of
activities have substantially exceeded initial expectations. Thus, the FFB has
become a central issue in recent debates about credit control.

The Need for Debt Management

By the early 1970s a large number of federal agencies had been authorized to
finance their operations through borrowing in the government securities market. This type of financing took several forms: sales of agency debt securities,
such as bonds or notes; sales of loans from agency portfolios; and sales of
bonds or notes to finance federally guaranteed loans. All of this was taking
place in addition to the Treasury Department's conventional marketing of securities to finance the government's debt.

The portfolio of federal securities offerings created problems in the government securities market. The 1972 report of the secretary of the Treasury noted
that "some Federal activity in the securities markets is occurring on roughly
two out of every three business days." [27] By the following year, as many as
eighteen different agencies and programs were participating in the securities
market. [28] The effect, according to Treasury officials and market analysts, was
both to overcrowd the market and to drive up the borrowing costs for federal
agencies. As one private analyst explained: "What's happening is that the
new agencies are crowding the financing calendar with issues whose purposes, credit terms, guarantees, sinking fund provisions and the like, cannot
be easily understood or appraised by investors. Many of these new issues are
of such small size that broad ownership appeal and distribution is not being
accomplished." [29] The unfamiliarity of the new securities, compared to those
regularly marketed by the Treasury Department, meant that a number of federal agencies found it necessary to offer interest rates well above those of the
Treasury to attract investors' funds. In addition, these agencies had to absorb
the administrative expenses of maintaining internal financing staffs or the
underwriting costs charged by private firms.

The immediate problem was a two-tiered system of debt management. For
Treasury Department securities, with full-faith-and-credit backing by the government, interest rates were quite favorable compared to general market rates.
For securities offered by other federal agencies, even with similar backing and
comparable maturities, however, interest rates were less favorable. The Treasury Department viewed this two-tiered system as a costly debt-management

problem, and it recommended the centralization of the marketing of securities issued or guaranteed by federal agencies in a Federal Financing Bank that would operate within the Treasury. In 1972 the Nixon administration sent this proposal to Congress. It was accepted by Congress the following year but with important modifications.

Budgeting and the FFB

In order to resolve the debt-financing problem, the Treasury Department was willing to continue existing practices relating to the budgetary treatment of credit programs. In testimony before the House Ways and Means Committee, Treasury Under-Secretary Paul Volcker emphasized this point: "The Federal Financing Bank is not a device to remove programs from the federal budget; nor is it a device to bring programs back into the budget. The Bank would in no way affect the existing treatment of federal credit programs." [30] What the Treasury Department did want, however, was authority for the secretary of the Treasury to review and approve or disapprove all agency proposals for new securities issues.

While the official justification for Treasury scrutiny was that it would facilitate more orderly federal borrowing, members of the House and Senate objected that such an authorization could be used as a type of impoundment to curtail or eliminate credit programs opposed by the administration. Responding to these objections, the Senate Banking Committee, which had jurisdiction over the FFB legislation, imposed deadlines for Treasury review and specified that no specific program could be disproportionately affected or curtailed by Treasury financing decisions. (Congressional concern over centralized control of credit by the executive branch has resurfaced during the Reagan administration, but its focus has shifted from the Treasury Department to the Office of Management and Budget.) During debate on the Senate floor, an amendment was added to exempt the Farmers Home Administration from requirements for Treasury Department approval. The House Ways and Means Committee added another important modification, exempting all guaranteed obligations from these requirements. While the Senate Banking Committee had earlier rejected such a blanket exemption, arguing that it could severely undermine efforts to coordinate federal borrowing, the Ways and Means version was eventually adopted, as were the review restrictions initiated by the Senate.

There were, then, clear indications of congressional expectations regarding the operations of the FFB. Its budgetary and programmatic effects were to be neutral. According to section 11 (a) of the FFB legislation, "nothing herein shall affect the budget status of the Federal agencies selling obligations to the Bank . . . or the method of budget accounting for their transactions." In addition, FFB financing activities were to be divorced from programmatic considerations. It would help to finance programs, not exercise discretion about their merit.

Finally, while the bank's charter provided that it could borrow only up to $15 billion from the public, it was authorized to borrow directly from the Treasury without limits. The assumption was that this latter form of borrowing authority would be used on an interim basis, allowing the FFB to obtain funds between regular public offerings of its own securities. These funds would subsequently be repaid to the Treasury.

Impact of the FFB

One of the earliest, and most important, disparities between design and practice emerged in the FFB's first and only attempt to auction its securities to the public in July 1974. As these issues were traded in the government securities market, interest costs turned out to be higher than those for comparable Treasury securities. This undercut one of the prime justifications for centralizing agency borrowings in the bank—insuring borrowing costs at the levels accorded Treasury securities. In response, Treasury officials in charge of the bank's operation decided that future borrowings would be exclusively from the Treasury.[31] Subsequently, when an agency with authorization to borrow funds came to the FFB, the bank would borrow the necessary funds from the Treasury, which would provide the funds at its current cost of borrowing. The bank would then charge the agency this interest cost plus a small premium (now at one-eighth of a percentage point) to cover administrative costs and contingencies. (Of course, the Treasury, in turn, had to increase its public borrowings to offset the funds channeled through the bank to the agencies.)

Restricting the FFB to direct Treasury borrowing has reduced the financing costs for federal agencies, which are assured of being able to obtain funds at rates nearly identical to those of the Treasury Department. At the same time, there is no limit on FFB borrowing from the Treasury. By the end of fiscal 1981, outstanding FFB holdings of agency debt and loans exceeded $100 billion, and annual net lending was running well above $20 billion (see Figure 3.1). Treasury financing has thus allowed the bank to evade the initial $15 billion ceiling on borrowing authority from the public and to do so without having to seek congressional approval for increases in the ceiling.

The volume of activity associated with the FFB, however, is only one aspect of its impact on credit programs. The assumption that the bank would not

Figure 3.1 Net Lending and Loans Outstanding of the Federal Financing Bank, Fiscal Years 1974–1983

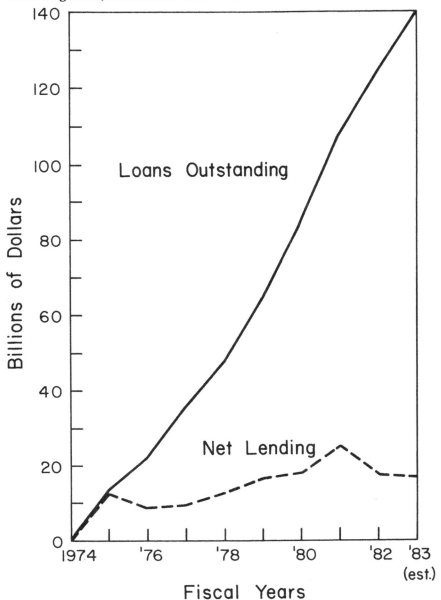

Source: *Special Analysis, Federal Credit Programs, Budget of the United States Government*, Fiscal Years 1976–84.

affect the budgetary treatment of credit programs, and therefore presumably would have no direct programmatic impact, has been only partially borne out in practice. The availability of FFB financing has, in fact, exacerbated problems of budget control that have long accompanied sales of loan assets and has introduced an additional difficulty by converting large volumes of loan guarantees into direct loans.

Problems of FFB Financing

Of the three forms of agency borrowing from the Federal Financing Bank, the smallest and least problematical is agency debt. In its simplest form, an agency with authorization to borrow funds in order to finance direct loan programs sells a bond to the FFB. The transaction between the agency and the FFB has no effect on the unified budget. Once the agency loans out the funds it has borrowed, however, the transaction is recorded as an outlay in its budget and is then reflected in budget totals. As shown in Table 3.1, most of the nearly $25 billion in FFB holdings of outstanding agency debt at the end of fiscal 1981 was accounted for by only two agencies—the Export-Import Bank and the Tennessee Valley Authority. This distribution has been characteristic of agency borrowing from the FFB since its inception; as the Export-Import Bank was switched from off-budget to on-budget status during the mid-1970s, the bulk of these transactions has been reflected in budget outlay totals.

The major growth in FFB financing, however, has not been in agency debt—although the increase here has been substantial—but rather in purchases of loan assets and guaranteed loans. As shown in Table 3.2, the increases in FFB holdings for each of these since the mid-1970s has far outstripped the growth in agency debt. More important, purchases of loan assets and guaranteed loans by the FFB—unlike purchases of agency debt—have important budgetary consequences. Their effect is to understate, by substantial amounts, direct lending, budget outlays, and the unified budget deficit and to distort apparent budget priorities.

Loan Assets and Certificates of Beneficial Ownership. The statutory provisions that allow the Farmers Home Administration and Rural Electrification Administration to treat CBOs as loan asset sales represent a serious budgetary inconsistency. The Federal Financing Bank, however, greatly increases the impact of this inconsistency. By providing ready funds for the purchase of CBOs, the bank allows the FmHA and REA to exploit with great effectiveness the statutory advantages they enjoy. FmHA direct loan programs, for example, grew relatively slowly over the more than two-decade period preced-

Table 3.1 Federal Financing Bank Holdings, Outstanding Agency Debt, Fiscal Years 1975–1983 (in billions of dollars)

	1975	1977	1979	1981	1983
On-budget Agencies					
Export-Import Bank[a]	4.0	5.9	7.9	12.4	14.7
Tennessee Valley Authority	1.4	3.9	7.1	10.9	13.1
National Credit Union Association	—	—	—	0.1	0.4
Off-budget Agencies					
U.S. Railway Association	0.0	0.3	0.4	0.2	0.1
Postal Service	1.0	2.2	1.6	1.3	1.1
Total[b]	6.5	12.3	17.1	24.9	29.1

Source: *Special Analysis, Federal Credit Programs, Budget of the United States Government*, Fiscal Years 1977–1984.
  a. Carried as off-budget agency in 1975.
  b. Totals are from the original data sources and may not equal column totals due to rounding.

Table 3.2 Outstanding Federal Financing Bank Holdings, Agency Debt, Loan Assets, Direct Loans, Fiscal Years 1976–1983 (in billions of dollars)

Fiscal Year	Agency Debt	Loan Assets	Direct Loans (purchases of loans guaranteed by agencies)
1976	10.0	9.2	3.1
1977	12.3	16.5	6.6
1978	14.2	23.3	10.5
1979	17.1	32.7	14.4
1980	21.1	40.4	21.5
1981	24.9	51.8	31.1
1982	27.8	57.2	39.3
1983	29.1	60.5	46.3

Source: *Special Analysis, Federal Credit Programs, Budget of the United States Government*, Fiscal Years 1978–85.

ing establishment of the FFB; since the FFB began operations, FmHA lending levels have soared (see Figure 3.2).

This extraordinary expansion, however, is not reflected in the FmHA's budget balances. While the annual volume of new direct loans increased roughly five-fold between fiscal 1974 and fiscal 1981—from $3.3 billion to $16.6 billion—the FmHA's reported net outlays went from $1.2 billion to $−1.9 billion, while its outstanding loans dropped from $3.2 billion to less than $1 billion. These figures are the result of CBO purchases by the FFB. Between 1974 and 1981 the FFB acquired almost $60 billion in CBOs issued by the FmHA (see Table 3.3). At the end of fiscal 1982 the FFB held over $50 billion in outstanding CBOs that had been purchased from the FmHA.

The budgetary treatment of CBOs, combined with FFB purchases, allows the FmHA to sustain high volumes of loan activity with no budget exposure. Of course, the government must borrow additional funds to finance the FFB purchases, but this borrowing is not part of the deficit for the unified budget. Thus, direct lending by the FmHA, which has ranged as high as $16 billion annually, is "repaid" by selling the on-budget loans to the off-budget FFB.

Loan Guarantees. Another method of disguising outlays occurs when the FFB purchases loans guaranteed by other agencies, thereby converting the guarantees into direct loans. With the agency guaranteeing full payment of principal and interest, the FFB will make the direct loan at interest rates only marginally above the cost of Treasury borrowing. There are more than a dozen agencies and programs receiving financing in this fashion, including two relatively large programs—foreign military sales and rural electrification. The FFB's outstanding holdings for these programs alone exceeded $27 billion at the end of fiscal 1982 and are currently projected to reach the $35 billion mark by the end of fiscal 1983.

The procedure for purchasing guarantees operates in a straightforward fashion, but the budget accounting does not. In the military sales program, for example, the Department of Defense issues loan guarantees to foreign governments to finance their purchases of U.S. military equipment. The foreign government then takes the loan guarantee to the FFB, which purchases it for the full amount of the guaranteed loan principal. The same procedure is used by the REA. The REA issues loan guarantees to rural electric cooperatives to finance construction of electrical facilities. The cooperatives then sell their guarantees to the FFB.

In each case, the borrower has received funds, in the form of a direct loan, from a federal source. Since loan guarantees are not considered to be budget authority or outlays, however, none of the loan activity is charged to the bud-

Figure 3.2 Direct Loan Disbursements, Farmers Home Administration, Fiscal Years 1951–1985

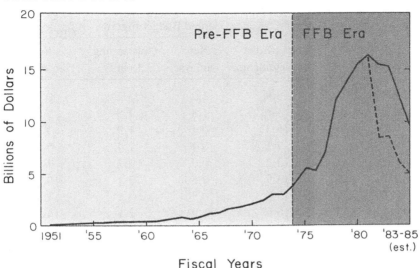

Source: Data for fiscal years 1951–77 are from Congressional Budget Office, *Loan Guarantees: Current Concerns and Alternatives for Control* (Washington, D.C.: Congressional Budget Office, 1979), pp. 36–39; data for fiscal years 1978–83 are from *Special Analysis, Federal Credit Programs, Budget of the United States Government*, Fiscal Years 1980–84.

Note: Figures for 1982–85 are reported separately for program loans and repurchases of loan assets. The dotted line for 1982–85 represents program level activity. The solid line is the total for program level activity and repurchases of loan assets, and it represents the appropriate comparison with prior-year activity.

Table 3.3 FmHA Lending, Budget Balances, and CBO Sales to the FFB, Fiscal Years 1974–1983 (in billions of dollars)

| Fiscal Year | Direct Loan Disbursements | Unified Budget Figures | | CBO Sales to the FFB |
		Net Outlays	Outstanding Loans	
1974	3.9	1.2	3.2	0.0
1975	5.6	−1.4	1.8	5.0
1976	5.3	0.1	1.9	3.8
1977	7.1	0.1	2.4	5.0
1978	12.2	0.3	2.7	7.7
1979	13.9	0.5	3.1	10.3
1980	15.8	0.9	4.1	11.4
1981	16.6	−1.9	2.1	14.5
1982	15.7[a]	−0.7	1.4	12.1
1983 (est.)	15.3[a]	0.7	0.8	10.8

Source: *Special Analysis, Federal Credit Programs, Budget of the United States Government,* Fiscal Years 1976–84.

a. Includes repurchases of loan assets.

gets of the Defense Department or the REA. Moreover, because the FFB is an off-budget agency, its direct loans—which are recorded as outlays—are not included in the unified budget's spending or deficit totals.

The growth in FFB purchases of loan guarantees has been extremely high in recent years. Outstanding holdings were less than $15 billion at the end of fiscal 1979 but more than doubled over the next two years and are expected to approach $60 billion by fiscal 1984. The annual outlay requirements have risen as well, from less than $4 billion in fiscal 1979 to an estimated $9.5 billion in fiscal 1983.

In addition to their aggregate impact on federal finances, FFB purchases of guaranteed loans have facilitated major program expansions. Direct lending by the REA, for example, has remained close to $1 billion annually since 1974. Direct loans by the FFB to REA-guaranteed borrowers, however, went from zero in fiscal 1974 to $4 billion in 1981. Foreign military sales have enjoyed a similar boost. FFB purchases of Defense Department guarantees averaged less than $2 billion annually from 1976 to 1979, but are expected to exceed $4 billion in fiscal 1983. These rather striking growth levels, which are characteristic of a number of programs in the loan guarantee purchase category, are particularly impressive in that they have taken place during a period of ostensible budget austerity. They are compelling evidence that budgetary procedures matter a great deal.

Distorting the Budget

The unified budget adopted in the late 1960s was designed to improve the accuracy and comprehensiveness of federal financial accounting. There was general agreement that such improvements were necessary to support effective scrutiny of programs within the budget process and to focus attention on the budget's macroeconomic effects. In presenting the unified budget to Congress, President Johnson expressed the hope that it "would assist both public and congressional understanding of this vital document." [32]

While the unified budget is still an important political document, its accuracy and comprehensiveness have been reduced by questionable accounting procedures. In particular, the Federal Financing Bank's funding of CBO sales and direct loans to guaranteed borrowers has modified substantially the spending priorities and fiscal policy reflected in the unified budget. From fiscal 1974 to fiscal 1981 more than $80 billion in spending was transferred off budget through CBO sales and loan guarantee purchases (see Table 3.4). Over the past several years, the outlay and deficit understatements in the unified budget have averaged more than $15 billion annually. With the deficit for the unified budget accounting for only part of the actual deficit—albeit the greater part— the control of fiscal policy becomes considerably more difficult.

The impact on spending priorities is equally important. In 1981, for example, FmHA disbursements exceeded $16 billion, with new loans financed through CBO sales to the FFB. As reported in the fiscal 1981 budget, FmHA outlays for the year were $-1.9 billion. If CBO sales had been treated as a means of financing rather than as negative outlays, the FmHA's budget would have looked quite different—$12.5 billion.

In the context of a fiscal 1981 budget of almost $660 billion, this may not appear terribly significant. In fact, FmHA spending was impressive even on a relative basis. "Proper" reporting of FmHA outlays would have placed the agency seventh among the fourteen cabinet-level departments and independent agencies when ranked according to size of budget. [33] Indeed, FmHA outlays were larger than those of nine of the seventeen *functional categories* in the budget. [34]

Some eighteen agencies and programs benefit from FFB financing in ways

Table 3.4 Outlay and Deficit Understatements Caused by FFB Financing, Fiscal Years 1974–1983 (in billions of dollars)

| Fiscal Year | Unified Budget Deficit | FFB-Financed | | Additional Budget Outlays/Deficit |
		Loan Asset Sales	Direct Loans to Guaranteed Borrowers	
1974	−4.7	0.0	0.1	0.1
1975	−45.2	5.1	1.0	6.1
1976	−66.4	4.1	1.9	6.0
1977	−44.9	5.1	3.0	8.1
1978	−48.8	6.8	3.9	10.7
1979	−27.7	9.4	3.9	13.3
1980	−59.6	9.4	6.8	16.2
1981	−57.9	11.5	9.4	20.9
1982	−110.6	5.4	8.7	14.1
1983 (est.)	−207.7	4.7	9.5	14.2
Total	−673.5	61.5	48.2	109.7

Source: Adapted from Congressional Budget Office, *The Federal Financing Bank and the Budgetary Treatment of Federal Credit Activities* (Washington, D.C.: Congressional Budget Office, 1982), p. 27. The 1982 and 1983 figures are from *Special Analysis F, Federal Credit Programs, Budget of the United States Government, Fiscal Year 1984* (Washington, D.C.: Government Printing Office, 1983), pp. F-26–F-29, and *Budget of the United States Government, Fiscal Year 1984* (Washington, D.C.: Government Printing Office, 1983), p. 9-55.

that disguise budget outlays. While the FmHA is the largest benefactor, the sums involved for other agencies are also significant. Programs that receive anomalous or inconsistent budgetary treatment enjoy a decided advantage in securing budgetary resources. They do not compete on an equal basis with direct spending programs, or even direct lending programs, for which outlays are accurately recorded. In fact, they may not have to compete at all. As long as FFB financing is readily available, rates of program activity are largely matters of agency discretion rather than executive or congressional action.

It is important to recognize, however, that these curious forms of budgetary treatment did not develop out of ignorance or in secrecy. Legislation was necessary to allow CBO sales to be treated as negative outlays. Legislative actions also determined that loan guarantees would be excluded from the definition of budget authority, and that the FFB would have off-budget status, unlimited borrowing authority from the Treasury, and no discretion over agency programs. These decisions were not theoretical exercises. They were designed to protect certain programs that enjoyed widespread political support. There might have been little appreciation in the early 1970s of the sums that would soon be channeled through the FFB, but there was an impressive amount of evidence readily available about the budgetary issues at stake.

It is not at all clear, therefore, that correcting inconsistencies in budgetary treatment would produce immediate and substantial cuts in currently protected programs. The political support for them is still very strong, which no doubt explains why the inconsistencies have not been corrected. At the very least, however, consistent accounting would eliminate some of the most serious distortions in the unified budget.

Improving Budget Accounting

As its volume of activity has increased, a good deal of criticism has been directed toward the FFB. There have been proposals in Congress to abolish the bank, to move it on budget, and to limit its purchases. While the bank has allowed agencies to finance substantial amounts of disguised spending, it is not the central problem. Its abolition or curtailment might simply drive agencies back to the private credit markets, with the resulting additional costs for borrowing that occurred during the early 1970s.

The real problems with the FFB are caused by the budgetary treatment of loan asset sales and direct loans to guaranteed borrowers. In both cases budget outlays are understated for agencies. Accurate and comprehensive budgeting would obviously require proper attribution of program activity to agencies and consistent treatment of program outlays. Legislation now pending in Congress would solve the attribution problem, and the Reagan administration has proposed that CBO sales be treated as borrowing. The prospects for the former appear much better than those for the latter, but both are necessary in order to place competing agencies and programs on a reasonably equal basis.

Chapter 4

Credit without Controls

The fiscal 1972 budget submitted to Congress by the Nixon administration declared that "reform of the budget process is long overdue" and identified as a major problem "federal credit programs which the Congress has placed outside the budget [that] escape regular review by either the executive or the legislative branch." [1] The president's budget message recommended "legislation to enable these credit programs to be reviewed and coordinated with other federal programs." [2] This recommendation received no follow-up, and the Nixon administration—like its successors during the 1970s—sponsored major credit initiatives while regularly deploring the absence of rigorous credit controls. For its part, Congress supported most of these initiatives, contributed its own creative uses of credit assistance, and, throughout the decade, agreed that the absence of comprehensive credit controls was indeed a problem.

The ambivalence that has typically characterized executive and legislative responses to credit assistance has some obvious explanations. There is no general agreement about how to measure the costs or to assess the economic impact of federal credit. In addition, the technical problems associated with budget accounting for credit are more complicated than those relating to direct spending. Most important, executive and congressional decision-making processes have tended to focus on specific needs for credit assistance rather than on aggregate or comprehensive credit policy. This tendency has been less pronounced during the past several years, particularly in the executive branch and most especially with the Reagan administration, but the absence of even rudimentary controls during the 1970s created an enormous array of programs, many of which continue to channel large sums of direct loans and loan guarantees. Credit without controls has meant, in effect, that credit policy is determined on a case-by-case basis rather than as part of a coherent approach to fiscal management.

Neither the executive nor legislative branch has been uniquely responsible— or irresponsible—in dealing with the economic implications of federal credit aid. Off-budget status has been extended to a variety of agencies, with no consistent rationale. Credit "bailouts" have been approved for farmers, corporations, and governments, sometimes after heated controversy but in other instances quite routinely. When budget reform was enacted in 1974, the effect was to exacerbate rather than lessen problems of credit control. The record of the 1970s illustrates that when credit politics and economics collide, the former usually wins. It shows as well that because the costs are indirect or hidden, credit assistance can be a much more attractive option than direct spending.

An Overview

As shown in Table 4.1, there have been approximately two hundred separate credit initiatives enacted since the mid-1960s, with particularly heavy activity from 1978 to 1980. (These represent only new programs or major revisions in ongoing ones. Simple extensions or funding changes are excluded.) Substantial credit aid has been channeled to most functional categories in the budget, although there has been a heavy concentration in agriculture and housing. Of particular importance, virtually every legislative measure prior to 1981 represented a major expansion of program activity or a liberalization of program eligibility. Only in the Omnibus Budget Reconciliation Act of 1981 were eligibility and program levels reduced in a number of functional categories.

Until very recently, then, the thrust of credit legislation has been expansionary, extending federal intervention to more and more sectors of the economy. While some bailouts, such as the Lockheed and Chrysler loan guarantee programs, have received substantial public discussion, considerably larger sums have been extended to other beneficiaries with relatively little attention. The loan principal of the Lockheed and Chrysler guarantees, for example, totaled $1.75 billion. The Federal Ship Financing Act of 1972 (PL 92-507) and the Emergency Livestock Credit Act of 1974 (PL 93-357) authorized loan guarantees of $5 billion but, along with most other credit measures, generated almost none of the scrutiny directed toward Lockheed or Chrysler.

What this suggests is that political and programmatic considerations, not fiscal or economic ones, determine credit policy. A review of some of the more important developments in credit policy reinforces this interpretation. And it shows why recent attempts to develop binding credit budgets have achieved such limited success.

Off-Budget Financing

The unified budget format adopted for the fiscal 1969 budget was not fully comprehensive. It did not include guaranteed loan transactions.[3] It also excluded the transactions of government-sponsored enterprises. The Commis-

Table 4.1 Credit Legislation Enactments, by Functional Category, 1965–1982

Year	Number of Measures	Major Initiatives by Function
1965	10	Agriculture, Education (Student Loans), Housing
1966	13	Disaster Relief, Participation Sales, Veterans Benefits
1967	7	Agriculture, Small Business
1968	16	Education (Student Loans), Foreign Assistance, Housing
1969	5	Disaster Relief, Education (Student Loans), Foreign Assistance, Housing
1970	17	Agriculture, Housing, Transportation
1971	9	Agriculture, Health, Small Business, Lockheed Loan Guarantees, Export-Import Bank Budget Exclusion
1972	8	Agriculture, Education (Student Loans), Transportation
1973	7	Agriculture, Foreign Assistance (Israel), Transportation, Federal Financing Bank
1974	8	Agriculture, Health, Housing, Export-Import Bank Budget Inclusion
1975	10	Agriculture, Energy, Housing, Transportation, New York City Assistance
1976	14	Area Redevelopment, Energy, Environment, Health, Transportation
1977	NA	
1978	23	Agriculture, Education (Student Loans), Energy, Health (Student Loans), Housing, Small Business, New York City Assistance
1979	18	Energy, Foreign Assistance (Israel-Egypt), Health (Student Loans), Transportation, Chrysler Loan Guarantee
1980	18	Agriculture, Education (Student Loans), Energy, Foreign Assistance, Housing, Transportation

Table 4.1 continued

| 1981 | 6 | Agriculture, Disaster Relief, Education (Student Loans), Energy, Housing, Small Business |
| 1982 | 7 | Commerce, Housing |

Source: *Special Analysis, Federal Credit Programs, Budget of the United States Government,* Fiscal Years 1967–84.

sion on Budget Concepts explained that, as a matter of policy, "government-sponsored enterprises [should] be omitted from the budget when such enterprises are completely privately owned."[4] Otherwise, the commission emphasized that the budget should "be comprehensive. . . . Borderline agencies and transactions should be included in the budget unless there are exceptionally persuasive reasons for exclusion."[5] Thus, with the exception of two government-sponsored enterprises—the Federal Land Banks and Federal Home Loan Bank Board—and the expenses of the Federal Reserve System Board of Governors, which were not funded by appropriations, the unified budget of fiscal 1969 included the spending and lending transactions of all federal agencies. The off-budget exceptions, however, soon became more numerous and considerably larger.

Government-Sponsored Enterprises

The categorical exclusion of government-sponsored enterprises from the budget assumed greater importance as additional lending institutions achieved full private ownership. During 1968 the Federal National Mortgage Association, Federal Intermediate Credit Banks, and the Banks for Cooperatives repaid the federal government's initial capital investment and moved from mixed to private ownership. The Farm Credit Administration (land banks, credit banks, and banks for cooperatives) was therefore entirely off-budget after 1968. In 1970 the Federal Home Loan Mortgage Corporation was established as an off-budget enterprise to provide an expanded secondary market for residential mortgages. Two years later, the Student Loan Marketing Association was created with the same status to provide additional funds for the guaranteed student loan program.

The government-sponsored enterprises have channeled substantial amounts of credit outside annual executive or congressional budget review. From 1970 to 1982 the total outstanding credit advanced by these institutions rose from approximately $35 billion to over $270 billion, with particularly high rates of

Table 4.2 Outstanding Credit Advanced by Government-Sponsored Enterprises, 1970–1982 (in billions of dollars)

	Net Loans Outstanding[a]		
	1970	1975	1982
Federal National Mortgage Association	13.4	29.1	76.9
Farm Credit System			
Banks for cooperatives	1.7	3.4	9.1
Federal intermediate credit banks	5.1	10.0	21.8
Federal land banks	6.5	15.4	50.5
Federal Home Loan Bank System			
Federal home loan banks	10.2	20.5	70.7
Federal Home Loan Mortgage Corporation	—	4.8	37.3
Student Loan Marketing Association	—	0.2	6.0
Total	36.9	83.4	272.3

Source: *Budget of the United States Government, Appendix; Special Analysis, Federal Credit Programs, Budget of the United States Government*, various years.

    a. Excludes loans between sponsored enterprises.

growth during the late 1970s (see Table 4.2). The original justification for excluding these enterprises from the budget, however, has yet to be seriously challenged.

Off-Budget Entities

If a legitimate case can be made for off-budget treatment of government-sponsored enterprises (that is, "private ownership"), no parallels can be drawn with regular government agencies, regardless of distinctions between spending agencies and credit agencies. Nevertheless, beginning in 1971, statutory off-budget exclusions were adopted for a number of agencies previously included in the budget and also for several new agencies. Most of these were credit agencies, but others, such as the Postal Service and Strategic Petroleum Reserve, were not.

    The first major exclusion was the Export-Import Bank (Eximbank), which was removed from the unified budget (and from statutory spending ceilings) in August 1971. Over the next several years, similar treatment was extended to the Postal Service Fund, the Rural Electrification Administration and Rural Telephone Bank, the Exchange Stabilization Fund, and the Housing for the Elderly or Handicapped Fund. During this period new off-budget agencies were created, including the Environmental Financing Authority,[6] the Federal

Financing Bank, the United States Railway Association, and the Pension Benefit Guaranty Corporation. The off-budget stratagem reached the height of its popularity during the mid-1970s. While several agencies were later returned to the budget, this has been partially offset by two recent additions—the Synthetic Fuels Corporation and the Strategic Petroleum Reserve (see Table 4.3). Of the seven current off-budget entities, all but two are credit agencies.

The moves to debudget and, in some cases, to rebudget agencies have always involved arguments about appropriate budgetary procedures, but these arguments have invariably been subordinated to cost and control issues. In fact, there has not been any consistency in employing off-budget treatment, and there appear to be no grounds to justify according off-budget agencies less rigorous review or control than that applied to on-budget agencies.[7]

Export-Import Bank. This last point is illustrated by Congress's treatment of the Export-Import Bank, which was returned to the budget three years after having been removed from it.[8] In 1970 a concerted effort was launched in the

Table 4.3 Current and Previous Off-Budget Agencies

Agency[a]	Fiscal Year Established/ Removed from Budget	Fiscal Year Returned to Budget
Environmental Financing Authority	1974	(authority expired 1975)
Exchange Stabilization Fund	1973	1980
Export-Import Bank	1973	1977
Federal Financing Bank	1975	—
Housing for the Elderly or Handicapped Fund	1976	1979
Pension Benefit Guaranty Corporation	1976	1982
Rural Electrification and Telephone Revolving Fund/Rural Telephone Bank	1975	—
Strategic Petroleum Reserve	1983	—
U.S. Postal Service	1974	—
U.S. Railway Association	1976	—
U.S. Synthetic Fuels Corporation	1982	—

Source: *Budget of the United States Government, Appendix*, Fiscal Years 1970–1984.

a. Does not include Federal Reserve System Board of Governors or Government-Sponsored Enterprises.

Senate, with Nixon administration concurrence, to move the bank off budget and thereby to prevent statutory spending ceilings from curbing its direct lending. The widespread pressure to expand bank lending was prompted by the deteriorating U.S. trade balance; also, supporters wanted to direct part of the expansion to the Soviet Union and eastern Europe by removing statutory bans on export financing for these countries.

According to the Senate Committee on Banking and Currency, budget restraints on Eximbank lending were unnecessary and inefficient:

> The flexibility which is required by the Bank to meet the demonstrated needs of the U.S. export community has been greatly curtailed since adoption of the unified budget concept under which the Bank's annual disbursements and receipts are included. . . . This budget restraint has deprived the Bank of the very flexibility it needs to support an increasing volume of exports at a time when the U.S. share of world trade is declining.[9]

The committee's report went on to point out that "Eximbank does not require appropriated funds."[10] Neither of these points were entirely accurate. The level of exports supported by the bank had almost doubled between fiscal 1969 and fiscal 1970—from $2.9 billion to $5.5 billion.[11] The appropriations argument neglected to mention that the bank had an initial capital stock of $1 billion, could borrow additional funds from the Treasury (up to $6 billion), and could also raise funds by selling its obligations in the private market. Treasury borrowing provided the bank with funds at a highly privileged rate of interest, and reserves accumulated over the years from undistributed profits added interest-bearing assets.

In any case, the support for expanding Eximbank lending was far too formidable to be successfully challenged on points of budgetary accounting. During House and Senate hearings in 1970 and 1971, representatives from banks, corporations, and executive agencies spoke almost unanimously in favor of "freeing" the bank. The only discordant note was struck by Comptroller General Elmer B. Staats, speaking for the General Accounting Office:

> In our view, excluding the Export-Import Bank's receipts and disbursements from the budget totals could establish an undesirable precedent . . . since it is impossible to differentiate between this loan program and other loan programs. . . .
>
> Our position is consistent with the conclusion of the President's Commission on Budget Concepts . . . that all loan programs operated by entities in which the capital stock is owned by the government should be included in the budget on a net lending basis.[12]

The only senator to push the GAO's position was William Proxmire, and his amendment to delete the off-budget provisions from the Export-Import Bank Expansion Act was defeated by a vote of 14–53. In the House a similar proposal sponsored by Charles Vanik was rejected 112–249. After several months of House-Senate disagreement over export financing for Communist-bloc countries, both chambers approved legislation allowing such financing, debudgeting the bank, and increasing the ceiling on outstanding Eximbank credit from $13.5 billion to $20 billion.

Three years later, the House and Senate cleared PL 93-646, which placed the bank back on budget, imposed restrictions on Soviet trade deals, and tightened congressional oversight regarding Eximbank financing of energy projects. This time the House-Senate roles were reversed, with the Senate pushing for statutory restrictions on bank activities and finally forcing the House to acquiesce. During the interim, Congress had written "limitations" on Eximbank program activity into annual appropriations acts. These had little effect, since net activity was usually well below the statutory ceilings and the lag time between commitments and actual disbursements was usually several years. What Congress did was simply include presidential estimates of program activity in its appropriations bills, with these estimates in turn being based on the bank's own projections.[13]

As either fiscal or programmatic control, this type of congressional check was clearly inadequate. When the bank's handling of export financing for the Soviet Union created major political embarrassments in 1973 and 1974, Congress acknowledged that programmatic review outside the annual budget process was unsatisfactory and reversed itself on budget treatment for the bank. Since the mid-1970s, Congress has lifted the ceiling on total outstanding credit—from $20 to $25 billion for fiscal 1975 and to its current level of $40 billion in fiscal 1979. Congress has also continued to include the annual limits on program activity, but these have usually matched administration estimates. The most important point is that Congress has periodically pressed the bank to tailor its lending decisions to political objectives, and similar pressures have come from the executive branch. In a 1976 analysis the Congressional Budget Office concluded that "Congress has used the Eximbank as a tool of foreign policy."[14] A more recent study reiterates this point: "Exim has not primarily pursued economy-wide objectives . . . [and] has not published any coherent analyses of its macroeconomic impact on the economy. . . . The bank does not work to stabilize overall U.S. economic activity, nor to balance the trade account. . . . In fact, Exim has been working at the level of the firm."[15]

The central questions about the Export-Import Bank involve costs and economic effects. Neither of these is illuminated very well regardless of the bank's budget status, since costs are in the form of implicit subsidies and economic effects are difficult to assess. Efforts to measure the subsidies involved in Eximbank lending reflect a host of methodological disagreements, but even the most conservative estimates are fairly substantial.[16] The Office of Management and Budget, for example, has estimated Eximbank direct loan subsidies as averaging almost $680 million annually for the period fiscal 1982–84, using a fixed market rate of 15.5 percent as a basis for assessment.[17] Congressional Budget Office estimates issued in the mid-1970s showed a slightly higher subsidy level with considerably smaller disbursements.[18] The office also reported that over 50 percent of the interest subsidies were accounted for by aircraft sales, nuclear power plant construction and equipment, and industrial machinery exports. Similarly high concentrations exist currently, with two-thirds of Eximbank's loans in 1980 serving seven companies. One of these—Boeing—had $5 billion of export sales in 1980, of which 60 percent included some form of Eximbank financing.[19]

The Reagan administration has been the first administration in almost two decades to challenge Eximbank financing precisely on this subsidy issue. Its efforts to use annual program limitations actually to reduce Eximbank activity were largely undercut by Congress for the fiscal 1981 and 1982 budgets, and recent estimates show substantial growth in guaranteed loan commitments through the late 1980s.[20] By focusing on credit subsidies, however, the administration has made it more likely that costs and economic impact will receive at least some attention.

The experience with the Export-Import Bank, then, shows that off-budget status reinforces assumptions that credit assistance is costless. The bank was moved off budget in order to facilitate program expansions without corresponding increases in outlays or deficits. It was returned to the budget in order to strengthen congressional influence over specific program decisions. While on-budget status undoubtedly increases the bank's visibility, it only reflects net lending and does not adequately address the fiscal implications of Eximbank programs.

Rural Electrification Administration and Telephone Bank. The unusual nature of Eximbank meant that its budget status was a critical control feature. The Rural Electrification Administration's loan programs were moved off budget in 1973 precisely as a protective measure. Congress was able to protect assistance programs that it supported. The Nixon administration was able to eliminate the effects of outlays for lending programs it opposed.

From 1965–1970, rural electrification and telephone loans averaged over $450 million in new commitments annually. In each of these years, Congress approved funding levels equal to or, in some cases, greater than those recommended by the executive branch. The largest add-on occurred in fiscal 1967, when the Johnson administration's proposed funding cuts of over $150 million in the two programs were rejected in favor of a $30 million increase.

The first budget submitted by the Nixon administration was a continuation of funding levels approved in previous years, and Congress responded with only a very small add-on in its agriculture appropriation bill. In fiscal 1972 and fiscal 1973, however, Congress added over $500 million to the administration's proposal for stable funding levels. The result was executive branch impoundments, and quite substantial ones. In fiscal 1973, for example, new commitments totaled $420 million, $320 million less than Congress had appropriated and even slightly less than the administration had initially recommended.

In 1972 and 1973 the president and Congress had additional disputes over several other rural assistance programs. Impoundments and veto threats were directed against the Rural Environmental Assistance Program (REAP), the Farmers Home Administration disaster loan program, and rural water and sewer grants. REAP was eventually restructured and incorporated into the 1973 omnibus farm bill. A veto of a new rural water and sewer grant bill was sustained by the House.

The FmHA program, along with REA, represented the major budgetary conflict. Legislation passed in 1970 and 1972 had established low-interest emergency loans for farmers and rural homeowners—three percent in 1970 and one percent in 1972—with forgiveness (or nonpayback) levels raised from $2500 to $5000. Under the 1972 law, demand for loans, and use of the forgiveness provisions, rose rapidly. Emergency loans during the first six months of fiscal 1973 were more than double the amount for any previous period, and the administration estimated that up to 75 percent of a projected $1 billion in loans during fiscal 1973 might need to be forgiven. On 27 December 1972 the Department of Agriculture announced curtailment of the program and impounded the remaining funds. One month later, the REA's direct loan program was unilaterally terminated and $367 million in appropriated funds was impounded.

The FmHA impoundment was declared illegal in March 1972 by a federal district court judge in Minneapolis, who ordered the program reinstated. One month later, however, legislation was approved by Congress that repealed the forgiveness provisions enacted earlier, increased the interest rate to 5 percent, and directed, rather than authorized, the secretary of agriculture to make disaster loans and designate emergency areas. In addition, the fiscal 1974 agriculture appropriation bill permitted the FmHA to sell certificates of beneficial ownership to the Treasury and to offset these against outlays. With this general protection for FmHA lending, new commitments for direct loans rose from $58 million in fiscal 1973 to $4.5 billion in fiscal 1975, while outlays in fiscal 1975 were $−1.4 billion.

The REA compromise followed similar lines, although outlays in this case were officially moved off budget. After terminating the REA direct loan program, the Nixon administration recommended it be replaced by a guaranteed or insured loan program administered under the Rural Development Insurance Fund of FmHA. The fiscal 1974 budget noted that this switch would "permit considerably higher loan levels [while] substantially reducing the outlay impact." [21]

Instead, Congress moved the direct loan program off budget. Amendments to the original REA act specified that all loans and advances issued by the agency "shall not be included in the totals of the budget of the United States Government." [22] It also authorized loan guarantees and specifically excluded these as well from the budget. Finally, agency borrowing that might be necessary from the Treasury, along with sales of existing loans to the Treasury, was exempted from unified budget totals.

Beginning with the 1974 agriculture appropriation bill, Congress also included language designed to insure that minimum levels for rural electrification and telephone loans would be obligated. The 1974 law set the permissible range for electrification loans at $618−750 million and for telephone loans at $140−200 million, while directing that any loan guarantees be in addition to those amounts. Minimum levels were subsequently raised to $750 million for electrification loans in fiscal 1976 and to $850 million in fiscal 1979, while telephone loans went to a $250 million minimum in fiscal 1976, which has been maintained since that time.

The Ford and Carter administrations did not challenge REA program levels, in large part because no direct budget outlays were at stake. President Carter did recommend that limits be set for guaranteed loan commitments in the 1981 appropriation bill for the Department of Agriculture and related agencies. Congress did not follow this recommendation in fiscal 1981, but did establish limits (and minimums) the following two years. At the same time, Congress refused to lower the direct loan minimums as recommended by the Reagan administration or to eliminate the "not less than" language it had used for the past decade to mandate lending.

Rural electrification and telephone loans have been so heavily subsidized that no pretense of costlessness is possible. The interest rate maximum of 5 percent set by the 1981 Omnibus Budget Reconciliation Act was well above the levels set for much of the 1970s but still considerably below the federal government's own borrowing costs.[23] The estimated subsidy for rural electric and telephone loans using a market-rate discount of 14.5 percent was almost $650 million in fiscal 1982 on $1.1 billion of new obligations or commitments.[24]

Unlike those of the Export-Import Bank, REA loan programs generated serious executive-legislative conflicts, and the off-budget solution was a successful attempt to resolve these conflicts. By moving outlays and additional deficit off budget, Congress was able to expand program activity while reducing the budgetary incentives for the executive branch to challenge program levels. For the REA, off-budget status has mattered a great deal.

Synthetic Fuels Corporation. With the obvious exception of the Federal Financing Bank, the Synthetic Fuels Corporation could eventually have the greatest budgetary impact of any currently off-budget credit agency. The corporation was created under the 1980 Energy Security Act to assist private industry in financing development of alternative fuel production. Financial assistance can take the form of direct loans, loan guarantees, price guarantees, or purchase agreements. Private firms are to own and operate alternative fuel plants, which are targeted to produce up to two million barrels of oil substitutes per day by the early 1990s from sources such as coal and oil shale.

The corporation's budget is not carried in the unified budget totals, but any funds needed for actual cash payments will be provided by the Treasury and recorded as on-budget outlays.[25] The original authorization for various forms of financial assistance totaled $20 billion. Up to $68 billion in additional assistance could be provided, however, if Congress approves the corporation's comprehensive plan scheduled for submission in 1984.[26]

Thus far, the Synthetic Fuels Corporation has not had large cash outlays; nor is substantial direct spending expected until the late 1980s. In fiscal years 1983 and 1984, however, loan guarantee commitments are expected to exceed $13 billion. As the 1984 budget states, additional outlays resulting from current and future guarantees are impossible to predict, but "may increase significantly up to the full amount of the loan and price guarantees."[27]

The uncertainty is related to the supply and price of oil. Alternative fuel production is much more costly than current oil prices. If this differential disappears, alternative fuels would be economically feasible and even profitable without government subsidy. If the differential remains or narrows only slightly, potentially enormous subsidies may be required. One of the three original synthetic fuels projects, the Great Plains Coal Gasification plant, has received $2 billion in loan guarantees. A profit of $1.2 billion originally projected by 1992 has turned into an estimated $770 million loss over the same period. The federal government is liable for the guaranteed loans, which translates into potentially large direct outlays.

With loan guarantees and risk of the magnitude involved in the synthetic fuels program, existing budget accounting procedures are clearly inadequate. The actual obligations that will result from current commitments cannot be estimated with any certainty. Moreover, while these obligations will ultimately be counted as on-budget outlays, the initial commitments are not affected by the budget authority ceilings contained in congressional budget resolutions. The effect of off-budget status in this instance, then, is primarily to shelter the synthetic fuels program from annual budget review and oversight.

Justifying Off-Budget Status

Legislative actions affecting the budgetary status of various executive agencies do not reveal a consistent pattern or persuasive justification. Two spending agencies are currently off-budget—the Postal Service Fund and Strategic Petroleum Reserve. For the Postal Service, all outlays are excluded with the exception of reimbursements charged to the Treasury for subsidized classes of mail. These subsidies amounted to $1.3 billion in fiscal 1981 and are estimated at $400 million for fiscal 1984.[28] Excluded is Postal Service borrowing, which is limited to $2 billion annually with a $10 billion ceiling. Indebtedness is estimated to reach $2.3 billion by the end of fiscal 1984.

The Strategic Petroleum Reserve was authorized in 1975, and financing was carried on budget through 1981. Outlays totaled approximately $6 billion during this period for storage facilities and acquisition costs. The Omnibus Budget Reconciliation Act of 1981 moved the acquisition costs off budget, producing "savings" of $3.7 billion for fiscal 1982 and a comparable amount for fiscal years 1983 and 1984.

In the case of the Postal Service Fund, off-budget status presumably accords with its intended businesslike operation and self-sustaining financing. It may also serve as a useful insulation from political pressures. Similar arguments cannot realistically be advanced concerning the Strategic Petroleum Reserve. And in both cases, substantial amounts of borrowing and outlays have been moved off budget, which suggests that budgetary incentives may be the primary explanation for these unified budget exclusions.

The off-budget status of credit agencies has at least some superficial plausibility. This plausibility rapidly disappears, however, when the major credit agency exclusions are examined. Exclusions have been enacted (and withdrawn) not because credit activities thereby function more efficiently but for specific programmatic purposes. Off-budget lending is not of a different character than on-budget lending, but it receives less congressional scrutiny. The same conclusion applies to off-budget spending.

For these reasons, the House and Senate budget committees have recommended that the off-budget protection extended to certain agencies be ended. In 1976, for example, the House Budget Committee stated that "there appears to be no convincing reason for continuing off-budget treatment of any . . . agencies except possibly the Federal Financing Bank where the budgetary treatment has to be considered in conjunction with the treatment of other agencies using the Bank." [29] Two years later, the committee renewed its recommendation that "appropriate legislative committees take prompt action to place all wholly owned off-budget agencies within the unified budget [and] to include the Federal Financing Bank in the budget." [30]

If progress with off-budget agencies has been limited despite the efforts of the budget committees, a serious reappraisal of the standard governing government-sponsored enterprises has been nonexistent. In this case, the budget committees have argued that the private ownership qualification can be achieved with relative ease, that this does not eliminate government involvement, and that it does not in and of itself justify removing credit enterprises from budgetary control by the executive branch and Congress. [31] The immediate moves to terminate mixed ownership for several agencies after the private ownership criterion was adopted in 1967 and the subsequent creation of new "private" enterprises suggests that ownership is, in fact, a minor consideration. And the current magnitude of credit activity for government-sponsored enterprises reinforces the need for either a total severing of government involvement or an integrated consideration of all federal credit activities.

The "Bailouts"

Off-budget agencies have managed to distribute billions of dollars in credit assistance while operating in relative obscurity, but considerably smaller sums directed toward single, large borrowers have aroused a good deal of controversy. The Lockheed, New York City, and Chrysler credit assistance programs—labeled "bailouts" by opponents—certainly have received much greater attention than most credit programs, but the controversy and attention have done little to clarify the economic costs or to develop a consistent rationale for federal intervention. Nor have these programs reflected ideological consistency, as liberals and conservatives switched positions on the various controversies, from Lockheed to New York City and Chrysler.

The single-borrower programs were not the only, nor even the riskiest or most expensive, bailouts undertaken during the 1970s. The extensive use of loan guarantees and other forms of credit aid was authorized for railroads, shipbuilders, and other industries dominated by large corporations. Small business credit programs proliferated and, as in the case of many agricultural credit programs, the smallness criterion was rather elastic.

The "covert bailouts" have been widespread and have involved substantial sums. The Maritime Administration's outstanding direct loans and loan guarantees, for example, totaled just over $700 million by fiscal 1970. Ten years later, the total was over $6 billion, and the fiscal 1984 estimate is over $7.4 billion. The Small Business Administration's outstanding direct loans increased from $1.5 billion by fiscal 1970 to $7.7 billion by fiscal 1980. During fiscal year 1980, official SBA defaults on direct loans and loan guarantees amounted to $580 million.[32] The Economic Development Administration's outstanding credit increased by over $1 billion during this period. Authorizations for the "new communities" program were raised to $700 million during the 1970s. None of the thirteen communities was financially successful, and the government was obligated to retire the outstanding guaranteed debt that peaked at $280 million by mid-1976.[33]

As for the overt bailouts, the effects and efficacy of federal intervention are not clear-cut. The piecemeal basis on which credit assistance has been extended to corporations has tended to focus attention on short-term survival and especially on maintaining employment levels. It is over a longer term, however, that profitability and employment levels are determined. And of course the truly difficult question is whether capital diverted by federal intervention would otherwise have created more jobs and greater economic growth. As one might expect, this question has been obfuscated by the several major bailout debates.

Penn Central and the Railroads

While the roster of federal bailouts usually begins with Lockheed, the first credit aid initiatives of the 1970s were designed for the Penn Central and other railroads in the Northeast and Midwest. Early in 1970 the Nixon administration proposed extending $225 million in loan guarantees to forestall bankruptcy by the Penn Central Transportation Company, the nation's largest railroad and sixth largest corporation. The initial design was to extend the guarantees under the Defense Production Act, which authorized their use to assist defense-related industries. This ran into immediate trouble in Congress, which included a provision in the 1970 Defense Production Act extension that prohibited granting more than $20 million in guarantees to any defense contractor without congressional approval.

Equally unsuccessful was an attempt to authorize $200 million in loan guarantees under separate legislation. The Penn Central Company responded by filing a bankruptcy petition covering its railroad subsidiary on 22 June 1970. One of the reasons that the early Penn Central proposals foundered was uncertainty about the potential size and cost of a rail assistance package. Original estimates ranged as high as $750 million in direct loans and loan guarantees to rescue the Penn Central and other railroads in similar condition. Moreover, a railroad loan guarantee program that had been set up in 1958 provided little optimism about potential losses. More than $240 million in guarantees was approved by the Interstate Commerce Commission for fifteen railroads. Several years after the program was terminated, almost $170 million in guaranteed loans had not been repaid.[34]

After bankruptcy had been declared, the rail unions added their support to the Penn Central's request for aid, and a $125 million loan guarantee program was approved by Congress on 30 December 1970. The Emergency Rail Services Act of 1970 authorized the secretary of transportation to guarantee loans for "any railroad undergoing reorganization under section 77 of the Bankrupty Act."[35] This meant, of course, the Penn Central. The "anonymous" beneficiary precedent was followed in the Lockheed legislation.

The congressional turnaround was explained in large part by the enforced settlement of a nationwide rail strike several weeks earlier. Congress approved legislation, requested by the president, to delay the strike. It also extended the delay from forty-five to eighty-one days and, on its own initiative, mandated a 13½ percent retroactive pay raise for the four hundred thousand members of railway operating unions. The House and Senate commerce committees, which reported the strike moratorium and pay raise legislation, sent the guarantee program to the House and Senate floors shortly thereafter and used the increased payroll costs to justify the credit assistance. This insured Democratic support, and the guarantee program easily passed both chambers.

Intervention in the rail industry soon increased, and rather substantially. The National Railroad Passenger Corporation (Amtrak), which was also set up in 1970 to operate a nationwide rail passenger system, received an initial federal grant of $40 million along with $100 million in loan guarantees. By the end of fiscal 1973 federal subsidies totaled $320 million and loan guarantee authority had been raised to $500 million. Ten years later the annual Amtrak subsidy was over $700 million and loan guarantee authorizations had been raised to over $900 million.

Amtrak was only part of the federal commitment. In 1972 Congress authorized $58 million in direct loans to the Penn Central and four other railroads. That same year, the repayment period on federally guaranteed loans was extended from fifteen to twenty-five years. In 1974 the United States Railway

Association (USRA) was established to design and finance a consolidated rail service system in the Northeast and Midwest. Initial funding levels were set at $550 million in authorizations and $1.5 billion in loan guarantees. These were soon increased, as the Consolidated Rail Corporation (Conrail) was approved in 1975 as a federally subsidized agency to take over the bankrupt rail systems. The fiscal 1976 supplemental appropriation bill provided $2 billion to finance the transfer to Conrail of properties owned by Penn Central and other bankrupt lines and also provided for forgiveness of $250 million in loan guarantees previously extended by the USRA. Along with continuing annual subsidies for Conrail, $150 million in new loan guarantees was authorized in 1979 and 1980 for the Milwaukee and Rock Island railroads.

The total federal investment required to keep the Penn Central operations in service, at greatly reduced levels, has been estimated at over $8 billion.[36] Conrail, which was to be profitable by the late 1970s, finally showed a modest profit several years later and is scheduled to be sold to private investors. Amtrak operations still require large annual subsidies.

The railroad bailout, then, has been neither modest nor conspicuously successful. Credit subsidies delayed but did not prevent the eventual abandonment of unprofitable lines or major work-force reductions. The direct costs of federal intervention have been considerable but sufficiently spread out and obscure to allow years of delay in shedding uneconomic operations.

Lockheed

Compared to the support eventually required for the Penn Central and other railroads, the Lockheed program was small ($250 million in federal loan guarantees), and the last of the outstanding guarantees was repaid by the end of fiscal 1977. As it did for the Penn Central, the Nixon administration took the lead in promoting credit aid, and there were attempts to broaden assistance well beyond Lockheed.

Lockheed's financial difficulties became apparent during 1970. A group of banks that eventually agreed to lend Lockheed $400 million to begin production of its new commercial airliner—the L-1011 Tristar—insisted on some form of federal protection, preferably loan guarantees. Instead, a special contingency fund appropriation of $200 million was added to the fiscal 1971 defense procurement bill to pay Lockheed for contested claims on the C-5A transport it was building for the air force. The effect was to enable Lockheed to meet its financing requirements while continuing to produce the C-5A.

Despite the additional funds, Lockheed's situation soon worsened. On 1 February 1971 the company agreed to accept a $200 million loss settlement as part of a new contract for the C-5A. Three days later, the engine supplier for the Tristar, Rolls-Royce, declared bankruptcy. On 13 May, President Nixon sent draft legislation to Congress calling for $250 million in loan guarantees for Lockheed. This federal commitment was demanded by Lockheed's creditors as necessary for extending additional credit, and this credit, in turn, was necessary to insure that the British government would finance a successor to Rolls-Royce to build the Tristar engines.

The primary administration spokesman for Lockheed was Treasury Secretary John Connally, who emphasized at the beginning what would be the dominant issue throughout the Lockheed debate—the unemployment repercussions of a Lockheed bankruptcy. Connally testified before the Senate Banking Committee that, counting the indirect impact, an estimated "60,000 employees will end up without jobs if the L-1011 is shut down." [37] He also noted that "credit assistance by the Federal Government is nothing new at all. One can cite many examples of ways in which the Congress has authorized credit assistance to various sectors of the economy." [38]

Hearings before the House and Senate banking committees took place during June and July. Domestic airline representatives, some of whom represented companies with large prepayments on the Tristar, and most labor union spokesmen backed the Lockheed guarantee, as did of course bank officials who had provided credit to Lockheed. There was, however, sustained criticism as well that the unemployment and bankruptcy fears were being exaggerated and, in particular, that a Lockheed rescue would set an unfortunate precedent.

This last point became more prominent as it became clear that there was considerable congressional support for a broad guarantee bill that would assist companies other than Lockheed. The Nixon administration, however, vacillated on the merits of a broad bill. Secretary Connally stated he would not "take a position in opposition to consideration of legislation of a rather broad and sweeping character." [39] He also suggested that "the time may have come in this country when we have to look at things somewhat differently [since] some of our corporations have now reached a size [that] defies the ability of traditional lending institutions to meet their demands." [40]

Deputy Secretary of Defense David Packard apparently had a different view. In a prepared statement that Packard attempted to withdraw but that House Banking Committee chairman Wright Patman read into the record, Packard declared he did not "support extending a broad Federal loan guarantee authority to the defense industry or any other industry at this time." [41] In fact, stated Packard, the Defense Department did not "need or want a broad loan guarantee bill which [would] only encourage a continuation of these practices which have caused this trouble."[42] And in an unusually candid fashion, Packard acknowledged that there were costs associated even with loan guarantees: "A Government guarantee for a particular company or a particular industry does not generate more credit for the economy. For example, this guarantee only diverts the credit the banks can offer someone else to Lockheed. We can afford to divert $250 million under the circumstances. To provide a mechanism whereby $2 billion could be diverted to firms in the defense industry or any other special industry is quite something else."[43]

Both committees nevertheless reported out broad guarantee bills. The Senate Banking Committee, which sent its proposal to the Senate floor on 19 July, recommended that up to $2 billion in guarantee authority be available for "large, well established, and credit-worthy enterprises" that experienced "difficulty in obtaining needed credit."[44] In a dissenting statement twice as long as the committee's justification, Senator William Proxmire charged that the general legislation was simply a ploy to make the "Lockheed bail-out . . . seem less odious and more respectable."[45] If so, the ploy was equally attractive to the House Banking Committee, which voted to substitute the Senate version for its own bill and to report the proposal to the floor.

Over the next two weeks the Senate failed three times to invoke cloture against a filibuster carried on by Senator Proxmire and other opponents of Lockheed aid. On 30 July the House passed an emergency guarantee bill, but only after adopting amendments that restricted it to the $250 million needed for Lockheed. The following day the Senate agreed to take up the House-passed version and to limit debate on the measure. On 2 August the Lockheed bill passed the Senate. The Emergency Loan Guarantee Act, which the president signed 9 August 1970, authorized guarantees "to major business enterprises" and nowhere mentioned Lockheed.[46]

The final votes on the Lockheed bill were extremely narrow. The House vote of 192–189 found majorities of Republicans (90–60) and southern Democrats (47–34) joined in support against a heavy majority of northern Democrats (55–95). A parallel liberal-conservative split occurred in the Senate, where the vote was 49–48. Republicans (27–17) and a slight majority of southern Democrats (9–8) barely prevailed against a 13–23 vote by northern Democrats.

An Emergency Loan Guarantee Board, consisting of the secretary of the Treasury, chairman of the Federal Reserve Board, and chairman of the Securities and Exchange Commission, had been created to administer the guarantee program, and commitments were made for the bulk of the guarantees by the end of fiscal 1973. Lockheed was able to repay the last of the guaranteed loans by the end of fiscal 1977. By early 1983 Lockheed was reporting record earnings, and prospects for its future profitability appeared excellent.

Whether this turnaround demonstrates the wisdom of the bailout is another matter. In 1981 the company finally decided to phase out L-1011 production, with losses on the aircraft totaling $2.5 billion. Over the preceding decade Lockheed had also lost its leading position as a defense contractor. And while the Lockheed rescue was not followed by a flood of corporate bailout appeals, it made it more difficult for Congress to resist expanding general credit assistance programs. If loan guarantees were costless in the Lockheed rescue, they would presumably be costless for others.

New York City

Supporters broke along a very different set of partisan and ideological lines when New York City requested credit aid in 1975. The Ford administration rebuffed the city's first request in May. By mid-October, as the prospects for default increased, the House and Senate banking committees began to consider legislation to guarantee bonds issued by New York to meet its expenses. President Ford announced his intention to veto the legislation, but one month later agreed to support direct federal loans.

During the interim the State of New York had stepped in to assist the city. In June the Municipal Assistance Corporation was created to sell long-term bonds backed by the state to pay off the city's short-term debt. By September the bond market's support had disappeared, and the state set up a board of overseers to direct the city's fiscal management and to administer state financing for short-term expenses. Despite those efforts, the city was close to default by October, and there was fear of a state default as well.

The House and Senate banking committees had attached a number of conditions to their loan guarantee proposals, including requirements that the state raise new taxes, the city balance its budget by fiscal 1978, and creditors agree to exchange short-term debt for long-term, lower-interest debt. When President Ford agreed to a direct loan program, the guarantees were dropped and additional conditions were imposed. A virtual wage freeze was mandated for municipal workers, city employee pension funds were required to extend $2.5 billion in loans, and supplemental state aid was incorporated. The Ford plan, which went directly to the House and Senate floors, called for up to $2.3 billion a year in seasonal financing, which New York City would be obligated to pay back at the end of its fiscal year.

Despite the president's support, congressional Republicans could not develop much enthusiasm for helping New York, just as liberal Democrats had found Lockheed assistance unacceptable. The House approved the direct loan proposal by a 213–203 vote with heavy majorities of Republicans (38–100) and southern Democrats (15–71) voting to reject the legislation, while northern Democrats (160–32) overwhelmingly supported it. Passage in the Senate was by a wider margin, 57–30, but only after cloture was invoked on 5 December. On 15 December the necessary supplemental appropriation was cleared to fund the direct loans.

Additional legislation was required the following year to allow the municipal pension funds to purchase city bonds without losing their preferential tax treatment. Congress also finally approved revised municipal bankruptcy laws that eliminated much of the confusion and uncertainty that had surfaced when a New York default was imminent.

The seasonal financing plan was utilized by the city to borrow $1.26 billion in 1976, $2.1 billion in 1977, and $2.0 billion in 1978. All of the loans were repaid on time, but as the aid program neared termination, city officials requested an extension and revived the earlier proposals for guarantees. With the Carter administration and House Democratic leadership supporting more aid, a $2.0 billion, fifteen-year loan guarantee program easily passed the House. The Senate Banking Committee, however, had earlier expressed its opposition to any further assistance, and it finally reported a smaller and more restrictive package than the House had approved.

Among the conditions contained in the conference agreement was a $1.65 billion ceiling on guarantees, a year-by-year scheduling of amounts, and a one-house veto provision for any guarantees after fiscal 1979. The agreement, which was accepted by both chambers, also required that by 1982 the city's budget be certified as balanced by independent auditors using "generally accepted accounting principles applicable to governmental bodies" and specified that federal guarantees could be used only for bonds purchased and held by city and state pension funds.[47] Finally, the legislation made guarantee authority contingent upon "amounts as . . . provided in advance in appropriation Acts."[48] The appropriations committees reported the necessary legislation, and the full program was in place by 20 September 1978.

By the end of fiscal 1982 outstanding guarantees for New York City loans totaled $1.4 billion. These are scheduled to decline to $0.6 billion by 1988 and to be fully retired by 1993. Since the restrictions included in the guarantee legislation are less stringent than those upon which direct loans were contingent, it is difficult to assess New York City's fiscal progress under the guarantee program. Federal aid did prevent a certain default in 1975, and the option at that time of municipal bankruptcy was made even less attractive by the inadequacy of existing statutes to cover the New York case. The aid extension, which had none of the urgency associated with the 1975 debacle, conversely generated much less conflict. If any general lesson can be drawn from the New York case, it is perhaps that decisions on credit have much less to do with general principles than with the beneficiary involved. Many conservatives who had no difficulty in understanding Lockheed's plight could find little sympathy for New York City. And many liberals who felt Lockheed should be made to pay the price for mismanagement were more than willing to explain how complicated fiscal responsibility really was when New York City was involved. It was probably of some significance as well that by 1978 a Democratic president and Democratic-controlled Congress were helping a state and city governed by the same party.

Chrysler

Since the Lockheed and Chrysler assistance programs fall into the category of corporate bailouts, it is easy to overlook some of the important distinctions between the two. The federal commitment in Chrysler's case amounted to $1.5 billion in principal guarantees, compared to the $250 million for Lockheed. With Chrysler, there was a serious effort to attach explicit, statutory conditions to the aid package, while contingencies for the Lockheed aid were almost nonexistent. The Chrysler guarantees were also long-term, with authority to continue until 1990, roughly double the Lockheed loan period.

The Chrysler scenario officially opened on 9 August 1979, when its management proposed that the Treasury advance to the company $1 billion for future-year tax credits. While this imaginative plan had no serious prospect for success, the request for aid was not dismissed out of hand. At the time, Chrysler was the nation's tenth largest corporation, with 130,000 workers in its domestic divisions and an annual payroll of more than $4 billion. While its automobile division had been shaky for many years, gasoline supply scares, new regulatory standards, and competition from foreign automakers intensified its difficulties during the 1970s. By 1979, Chrysler was registering huge losses. Indeed its $720 million loss during 1979 represented one of the largest losses in U.S. corporate history.

Three months after Chrysler's tax credit scheme failed, the Carter administration agreed to sponsor a $1.5 billion guarantee program, contingent on Chrysler's getting matching nonguaranteed financing. Over the next seven weeks, congressional debate proceeded along two tracks. First, there was an occasional attempt to put the Chrysler proposal into the context of general principles—free enterprise versus federal intervention being the most common. Second, there was a much more important debate over the conditions that would be attached to federal guarantees. Among these, the key point was the extent of wage concessions to be made by Chrysler employees.

President Carter's aid package accepted as a sufficient employee contribution the $203 million differential between the United Auto Workers' contract with Chrysler and its contracts with Ford and General Motors. The president's plan did not specify how matching financing for the guarantees was to be raised, and it placed all administrative authority for the guarantee program with the secretary of the Treasury. The House Banking Committee endorsed the administration's proposal two weeks after it was submitted, but postponed reporting out a bill while the Senate Banking Committee developed its version.

The Senate bill, which was reported out of committee on 29 November by a 10–4 vote, differed on a number of important points from the Carter-House measure. It contained considerably greater detail about the required sources of matching financing, placed administrative authority in a board rather than solely with the Treasury secretary, and, most important, made the entire aid package contingent on a wage freeze for Chrysler employees. When the UAW strenuously opposed this, it took three weeks to work out a compromise between the House and Senate.

Floor action in the House was completed rapidly. The argument that a Chrysler bankruptcy would cause massive job losses was never seriously challenged, although there were quite disparate assessments of what those losses might actually be. House Speaker Thomas P. O'Neill took the floor to claim that up to 700,000 people might lose their jobs if Chrysler went under.[49] He also declared that the eventual taxpayer costs of a Chrysler bankruptcy could be as high as $4 billion in additional spending and lost revenue. Representative David Stockman attempted to revive what he described as "serious arguments" about the consequences and real costs of federal intervention, and he charged that these arguments were being subordinated to the upcoming electoral calendar.[50] The House Democratic leadership did agree to a modest increase in employee wage concessions, to $400 million, and the Chrysler measure passed by a 2–1 margin.

It was assumed that the overwhelming support shown in the House would force the Senate to modify its wage concession requirements. This assumption proved correct, as the Senate adopted by a 54–43 vote an amendment to the original banking committee bill that reduced the wage freeze to the $400 million in wage concessions voted by the House. Opponents of the aid threatened a filibuster, however, and they succeeded in having the figure raised to $525 million. During conference House and Senate conferees split the difference exactly in half.

The aid package as cleared on 21 December authorized $1.5 billion in guarantees, with $2 billion in matching "contributions" from workers, dealers, creditors, and state and local governments. The wage concessions by union workers still left an estimated $600 million in raises over a three-year period, and the concessions were partially offset by distributions of new common stock. The legislation simply required "adequate assurance" of matching commitments, not legally binding ones, before guarantees could be extended to Chrysler.[51] However, an important restriction that was preserved in the final measure was a prohibition against Federal Financing Bank purchases of the loan guarantees. This prevented federal conversion of the guarantees to direct loans.

As with the New York City guarantees, the Chrysler authorization required appropriations action.[52] This was intended to provide an additional control point for loan guarantees by voting them through the appropriations committees as well as the authorizing committees. Just how much control this represented can be judged from the House and Senate floor debates. The "urgent appropriation" was cleared by Congress the same day as the authorizing bill. It set the loan guarantee total at $1.5 billion "of contingent liability for loan principal and for such additional sums as may be necessary for interest payments."[53] Members who thought that the government's maximum liability was $1.5 billion now found that there was an indefinite additional liability. On the House floor the chairman of the appropriations committee, Jamie Whitten, conceded that the government's exposure could be well in excess of $1.5 billion, but was unable to estimate what that additional exposure might be.[54] When Robert Bauman, an opponent of the aid program, reported that "interest payments alone could cost more than $4 billion," his figure was not challenged, but the House immediately moved to approve the appropriation measure.[55]

Despite the highly publicized conditions attached to Chrysler aid, there was no ceiling on the government's liability. Nor were the final conditions especially stringent. The first installment of guarantee commitments, $800 million, was made early in 1980. An additional $400 million was issued in fiscal 1981, and the maximum level of outstanding guarantees reached $1.2 billion, well below the statutory ceiling. Chrysler was able to pay off its outstanding guarantees in August 1983.

Federal loan guarantees undoubtedly prevented a Chrysler bankruptcy, and by early 1983 Chrysler was showing a profit. Hardly mentioned is the fact that its work force has declined by over 60,000 jobs, or nearly one-half, since 1968. Nor is it clear that Chrysler's profitability can be maintained without import restraints against foreign automobiles or in the face of new wage concessions.

Bailouts as Policy

The Lockheed, New York City, and Chrysler credit assistance programs are conspicuous because they are large, single-borrower cases. They illustrate, however, the almost complete absence of a coherent federal credit policy, an absence that is even more striking when the less conspicuous covert bailouts are examined. For Lockheed, New York City, and Chrysler, it is highly unlikely that direct aid, in the form of grants or explicit subsidies, could have been approved. Loan guarantees, however, were treated as cost-free and were therefore a feasible alternative.

The perception that loan guarantees entailed no cost was reinforced by the absence of any fiscal tradeoffs. Without comprehensive credit controls, guarantees and even direct loans could be handled on a piecemeal basis. And with guarantees, there was no problem with the spending ceilings in congressional budget resolutions. Absent even these minimal constraints, it should not be surprising that short-term political considerations dwarfed the long-term economic ones.

Budget Reform and Credit

The relationship between credit programs and budget control was not exactly an unexplored topic when Congress commenced its budget reform deliberations in 1973 and 1974. The Commission on Budget Concepts had identified many of the shortcomings in the handling of federal lending activities. Off-budget status was being approved for formerly on-budget agencies, large amounts of direct lending were being shifted off budget, and loan guarantees were proliferating.

The Joint Study Committee on Budget Control, which reported the first and most restrictive budget reform proposal, responded to the loan guarantee problem by recommending that guarantees be treated as budget authority. This would have made the guarantees subject to targets and ceilings in congressional budget resolutions. The Senate Rules and Administration Committee, which revised the original budget reform measure, recommended that off-budget status for regular agencies be terminated.

Neither of these recommendations was approved, and the result was a deliberate bias in the new congressional budget process.[56] Off-budget outlays and debt, while obviously not "free" according to any rigorous fiscal standard, were free as far as congressional or executive budget totals were concerned. Loan guarantees were even more attractive. They were not subject to any aggregate ceilings, and their subsidy costs and indirect economic costs did not have to be estimated.

Congressional budget reform did focus greater attention on spending totals, but this had the perverse effect of increasing the incentives to distribute aid in the form of credit. The 1970s, then, provided an experiment in credit policy *deliberately* without controls. The results show not just the predictable expansion but the failure to address in any serious fashion the substantive issues relating to federal allocation of credit. By the end of the decade the scope of federal credit activity was so great that credit control problems could no longer be ignored, and the executive branch and Congress finally began to explore how more effective control might be achieved.

Chapter 5

The Credit Budget—
Information versus Enforcement

The scope and growth of federal credit activity during the 1970s generated widespread support for a credit control system. Executive budgets during the Ford and Carter presidencies assigned an increasingly prominent place to what were labeled "fiscal activities outside the federal budget," and, beginning in 1977, focused on specific credit control proposals. As the budget committees achieved success in institutionalizing the congressional budget process, they began to consider integrating spending and credit budgets.[1] Budget support staffs, including the Congressional Budget Office, General Accounting Office, and Office of Management and Budget, along with the Federal Reserve Board, unanimously endorsed a comprehensive credit control system.[2]

In sum, credit control was assuming full-fledged status as a "good government" issue. A series of congressional hearings, for example, evidenced widespread agreement that the uncontrolled growth of federal credit posed serious, if perhaps obscure, problems for federal economic management efforts. There was the occasional reservation that housing or agriculture or some other program area was a "special case," but these reservations were typically offered in the context of general support for stronger credit controls. As the House Budget Committee concluded: "Despite the inherent difficulties involved in developing a credit control mechanism, the committee believes that the problem of uncontrolled and uncoordinated Federal activities in this part of our overall fiscal policy sphere is a serious shortcoming in the congressional budget process and . . . the development of such a mechanism is crucial to the evolution of the budget process."[3]

Nevertheless, progress in developing a comprehensive and enforceable credit budget during the Ford and Carter administrations was quite limited. The legislation necessary to make basic changes in budget-accounting practices and congressional procedures never advanced very far. By the end of Jimmy Carter's term, there was a federal "credit budget" and accompanying control system, but its impact on credit policy was extremely modest. In Congress, the budget committees' enthusiasm for extending their jurisdiction to credit was tempered by their fear of opening the 1974 budget act up to other, less favorable, revisions. As a result, credit targets were finally included in budget resolutions but were not enforceable against authorizing or appropriations committees that had jurisdiction over direct loan and loan guarantee programs.

Plausible explanations for the lack of progress are not hard to fashion. While credit budgets had a definite appeal for budget experts, this appeal could not be translated into public understanding or support, given the complexity of the issue. Further, although presidents Ford and Carter perhaps brought a good deal of sincerity to budget reform, neither was particularly consistent in dealing with federal credit intervention. Unlike the clear-cut antiinterventionist stance of the Reagan administration, credit control during the Ford and Carter presidencies was to a considerable extent an abstract issue, largely divorced from any wholesale assault on the rationale behind, and programmatic expressions of, federal credit policy. Given this, attempts to curb credit growth were not pursued with great zeal and were eventually subordinated to efforts to reduce spending and deficits.

Another reason that credit control progressed very little was that it required resolution of difficult substantive issues. There was the general problem of off-budget entities with their policy-based statutory exclusions. Among the off-budget entities, the Federal Financing Bank posed unique attribution and control problems. Loan guarantee programs were not in most instances subject to annual limits and in a number of authorizing statutes were not subject to any limits at all.[4] Open-ended statutes were used by authorizing committees to encourage, not discourage, increased levels of program activity. Finally, government-sponsored enterprises presented a serious dilemma. As they were privately owned, they were not included in the annual budget process. Because they were government sponsored, however, their financial schedules were reported in the budget appendix. There were occasional intimations in executive and congressional budget materials that, whatever merit the distinction between ownership and sponsorship had once had, the sheer magnitude of activity by these enterprises could no longer be ignored. Neither the executive branch nor Congress was able, however, to devise appropriate and acceptable controls.

The Ford and Carter years, then, were a transition period in the treatment of federal credit. More attention was directed at the growth of federal credit. Review and monitoring of credit programs were strengthened. Decision-making processes in both branches were improved. Credit policy, however, was barely affected.[5] The credit budget mechanism that took several years to develop provided neither the centralized control nor procedural enforcement necessary to direct credit policy. Like effective spending control, credit control proved to be elusive. Indeed, the difficulties associated with spending control exacerbated the problems related to credit.

The Executive Credit Control System

The first broad effort to resolve the growing problem of credit control was incorporated by the Ford administration in its fiscal 1978 budget proposals. President Ford recommended two immediate legislative initiatives aimed at the off-budget financing of lending programs. His first recommendation was to repeal the statutory exclusions for *all* off-budget entities effective with the fiscal 1979 budget.[6] The second dealt with certificates of beneficial ownership, requiring that loan sales through these or similar financial instruments be treated as borrowing and not as offsets against outlays.[7]

A third recommendation was less forthright. Noting that Congress had deliberately excluded loan guarantees from budget authority ceilings under the 1974 budget act, the administration suggested that "this decision deserves reconsideration."[8] Also included was a more general change in the executive and legislative budget processes—a proposed three-year cycle to replace the annual budget.

Since President Ford left office shortly after submitting his fiscal 1978 budget, there was no serious follow-up on any of these measures. Carter administration officials subsequently agreed that a credit control mechanism was necessary and pledged to "work closely with the appropriate committees of the Congress to reach agreement on a mutually acceptable system."[9] In its fiscal 1979 budget the administration suggested that consideration be given to complementary controls in the executive and congressional budget processes "including ceilings on aggregate lending activity" and "limitations in annual appropriations acts on the amounts of new direct loans and loan guarantees for each [credit] program."[10] The only Ford proposal to receive specific endorsement was the three-year budget cycle.[11] Indeed, multiyear budgeting in various forms soon became a staple of budget reform proposals, a development which reflected the growing difficulties with year-to-year budget control and which, like the credit budget that later appeared, sought a procedural solution for a policy problem.

It is worth noting that the Carter approach to federal credit was directed primarily toward integrating credit policy with overall economic management. The fiscal 1979 budget emphasized that systematic, comprehensive treatment of credit programs was necessary "to influence efficiently the allocation of economic resources and the behavior of financial markets and the economy as a whole." [12] This exuberant endorsement of federal economic management, then, assumed the efficacy of credit intervention.

The Credit Budget

The basic outlines of an executive credit control system were described in 1978, but it took two more years to develop a formal credit budget. The fiscal 1980 budget simply announced that the administration would establish a more thorough credit monitoring and review process and restated the framework within which complementary executive and congressional controls could operate. Finally, in his fiscal 1981 budget, President Carter proudly announced implementation of "a system to control federal credit activities." [13]

The system had two major components. First, it included a recommended ceiling for aggregate credit during the fiscal year—new direct loan obligations by on-budget and off-budget agencies along with new loan guarantee commitments. The ceiling on gross credit activity, rather than on net changes, established a point of control that would not be affected by unanticipated changes in repayments, expirations, or other adjustments in previously extended credit. Second, in order to enforce the ceiling, annual limits were proposed for individual programs in the form of appropriations bill provisions.

This system required congressional cooperation. It presupposed that the budget committees could add aggregate credit totals to congressional budget resolutions. It also assumed that the appropriations committees would observe these totals by setting limits on authority to lend or to guarantee loans for each budget account under which credit activity was administered. The former was possible since section 301(a)(7) of the 1974 budget act provided that budget resolutions could include "such other matters relating to the budget as may be appropriate." [14] Since off-budget entities and loan guarantees were not covered in the enforcement sections of the budget act, however, the budget committees lacked the procedural leverage to induce compliance by the appropriations committees. As for the appropriations committees, some annual program levels had been included in appropriations bills in the past, but these had generally been aimed at protecting program activity against unilateral executive branch reductions. It was unclear, therefore, whether the appropriations committees would be willing to risk antagonizing authorizing committees by curbing credit program activity.

There were also major loopholes in the control system's coverage. Lending by government-sponsored enterprises, for example, was entirely excluded.

Loan guarantee figures (aggregates and individual program levels) were limited to the government's contingent liability, not based on the full principal of the guarantee. For the estimated federal credit for fiscal 1981, these exclusions represented almost $100 billion, or more than 40 percent of total credit advanced under federal auspices.[15] With respect to net lending, the exclusions represented about one-third of federally assisted credit for fiscal 1981 (see Table 5.1).

These exclusions were generally consistent with prior credit-accounting practices, so they were not unexpected. What was surprising, however, was the administration's decision to request annual program limits on a highly selective basis. Emergency credit assistance and credit insurance programs, for example, were exempted from appropriations bill ceilings, as were credit programs administered as entitlements. The administration argued that annual limits would not be effective for emergency programs or entitlements. The exceptions for housing credit and agricultural export credits were defended on general economic grounds.

As shown in Table 5.2, the programmatic exemptions within the credit control system accounted for approximately 55 percent of new direct lending and 60 percent of new loan guarantee commitments. Ensuing criticism from budget committee spokesmen of the scope of these exemptions led the administration to propose marginal increases in appropriations controls, especially for loan guarantees, in its first series of fiscal 1981 budget revisions. It suggested, however, that any substantial expansion of annual credit controls through the appropriations process would not be possible or desirable. James T. McIntyre, director of the Office of Management and Budget, explained to the House

Table 5.1 Net Federal Credit and Federal Credit Control, Fiscal Year 1981 Estimates (in billions of dollars)

Net federal and federally assisted credit	71.2
Exclusions from credit control system	24.4
Government-sponsored enterprise loans	(13.8)
Nonguaranteed portions of federally guaranteed loans	(8.8)
All other exclusions	(1.8)
Net lending and loan guarantees in credit control system	46.9
New direct loan obligations	(16.0)
New loan guarantee commitments	(30.9)

Source: *Budget of the United States Government, Fiscal Year 1981* (Washington, D.C.: Government Printing Office, 1980), pp. 19, 81.

Table 5.2 Appropriations Bill Limitations, Fiscal Year 1981 Estimates

	Requested Appropriations Bill Limitations	Exempt from Limitations	Total
New direct loan obligations	$27.2	$33.5	$ 60.7
New loan guarantee commitments	32.5	48.9	81.4
Totals	$59.7	$82.4	$142.1

Source: *Budget of the United States Government, Fiscal Year 1981* (Washington, D.C.: Government Printing Office, 1980), pp. 20–21.

Budget Committee that credit would eventually be handled through a "multi-year budgeting process. We will try to phase this [control] program in, until we get a much better handle on credit programs in the federal budget." [16]

There was additional criticism of the effect that uncontrolled programs might have on lending by the Federal Financing Bank. The Carter credit budget did not directly limit FFB activity, but instead relied on program-by-program limitations. Since these limitations were not, in the case of exempted programs, tied to appropriations controls, FFB activity levels were potentially open-ended. Even without this loophole, moreover, FFB lending could not be controlled in a given year, except to the extent that there was an enforceable ceiling on total federal credit activity. According to the Congressional Budget Office, "The failure of the Administration to propose limitations on actual FFB activities means that opportunities to manipulate unified budget totals through off-budget credit activity [would] remain uncontrolled." [17]

The proposed aggregates for fiscal 1981, moreover, projected substantial growth in credit activity, even for those programs subject to the credit control system. Outstanding federal credit, for example, was estimated to increase to just under $430 billion for fiscal 1981, 12 percent over fiscal 1980 estimates and 27 percent over fiscal 1979 levels. By comparison, the spending budget initially submitted for fiscal 1981 showed a growth rate for outlays of 9 percent over the preceding year and 24 percent for the fiscal 1979–81 period.

Credit growth was to be accommodated, however, in ways that would not adversely affect spending budget totals (see Table 5.3). On-budget direct loans were to be cut sharply, so that net lending for fiscal 1981 would actually produce negative outlays. Off-budget net lending would be maintained at fiscal 1980 levels, while net loan guarantees would be increased by 25 percent.

Table 5.3 Outstanding Federal Credit and Net Federal Credit, Fiscal Years 1979–1981 (in billions of dollars)

	FY 1979	FY 1980 (est.)	FY 1981 (est.)
Outstanding Credit			
Direct loans			
On-budget	79.9	85.4	84.8
Off-budget	57.5	74.2	90.8
Loan guarantees	197.7	222.3	253.2
Totals	335.1	381.9	428.8
Net Lending			
Direct loans			
On-budget	5.0	5.5	−0.6
Off-budget	13.6	16.6	16.6
Loan guarantees	19.0	24.7	30.9
Totals	37.7	46.8	46.9

Source: *Budget of the United States Government, Fiscal Year 1981* (Washington, D.C.: Government Printing Office, 1980), pp. 18–19.

Control versus Reduction

The Carter credit budget, then, did not equate control with reduction. In this sense, it resembled the ostensibly neutral spending budget reforms of 1974. Comprehensiveness and coherence were to be substituted for piecemeal consideration. There was to be more and presumably better information on which to base decisions. But controls could be used with equal ease to direct higher or lower program levels. Indeed, with credit programs, the bias in favor of higher levels was pronounced, since congressional inaction meant essentially no annual limits on aggregate credit activity.

Further, there was no particular rationale advanced for the credit aggregates recommended in the Carter budget. No attempt was made to analyze the potential macroeconomic effects of given credit levels or to distinguish between credit programs on the basis of economic effects or subsidy costs or risks. The aggregates simply reflected prior-year credit levels, and the mix between on-budget loans, off-budget loans, and guaranteed lending was largely a function of their relative budgetary effects.

It can be argued that the limited scope of the first formal credit budget was a tactical concession to supporters of credit programs in Congress who would have fought any serious attempt to centralize credit program controls. In this sense, establishing the precedents for credit aggregates and appropriations controls was more important than attempting to curtail credit activity. This does not explain, however, why it took three years to formulate a credit budget that was described by the Congressional Budget Office as "a cautious first step." [18] Nor does it explain why the credit budget was least effective in controlling the most rapidly growing forms of credit—off-budget lending and guaranteed lending.

A more persuasive, if equally inferential, case can be made by relating the credit budget to the general budgetary situation at the beginning of 1980. In fiscal years 1978 and 1979, budget outlays and deficits were well under the high growth rates projected in Carter administration and congressional budgets. The fiscal 1979 deficit, for example, was about half that originally estimated in the president's budget and in Congress's first concurrent budget resolution. The fiscal 1980 budget was another story. When fiscal 1980 budget planning began, the executive branch and Congress attempted to reduce substantially the rate of growth in spending. Indeed, the estimated outlay growth for fiscal 1980 was just more than half that projected the prior three years. This was the first serious attempt at budget restraint, and it was motivated, in part, by the spending shortfalls that had occurred during the fiscal 1977–79 period.

Well before fiscal year 1980 began, however, it was obvious that spending growth would be much higher than anticipated. Congress was forced to raise its outlay ceiling by $15 billion in the second budget resolution for fiscal 1980, and there was widespread agreement that additional—and probably larger—increases would be required during the fiscal year. Thus, as the fiscal 1981 budget was entering its final preparatory stage, spending and deficit control problems were becoming severe. In addition, inflation rates were climbing rapidly, generating even more political pressure to reduce budget deficits, while at the same time forcing up budget outlays.

When the Carter administration submitted its fiscal 1981 budget, therefore, congressional attention was focused almost exclusively on the outlay and deficit totals. Convinced that another deficit budget would be difficult to defend in an election year, the Democratic leadership in Congress directed the president to come up with a balanced budget. The quickly revised Carter budget for fiscal 1981 was not only balanced but showed a $16 billion surplus. The first concurrent budget resolution adopted by Congress was also a surplus budget. In fact, neither the Carter nor congressional budgets had any serious prospect for balance, although Congress refused to acknowledge this until several months after the election when it raised the fiscal 1981 spending ceiling by almost $50 billion and changed the surplus to a $60 billion deficit. [19]

In just two years, fiscal 1980 and 1981, the president and Congress underestimated budget outlays by nearly $100 billion and the unified budget deficit by an equivalent amount. Under these circumstances, credit control was not a high priority. Moreover, there was little sentiment in either the executive branch or Congress to exacerbate on-budget problems by changing the treatment of off-budget spending. With the "real" budget seemingly out of control, it was not at all surprising that the credit budget was pushed so tentatively.

The Congressional Response

The Carter credit control system drew a mixed (and muted) response in Congress. For committees whose jurisdictions were slated for expansion, namely the budget committees and appropriations committees, the reaction was generally supportive. The authorizing committees, which had always resisted centralized spending control, were not enthusiastic, especially when it came to programmatic limits.[20]

The 15 March views and estimates submitted to the House and Senate budget committees reflected these different viewpoints. In the House, for example, the appropriations committee declared that "bringing all credit programs into the budget process will help coordinate credit policy with fiscal policy, and help synchronize the allocative aspects of Federal credit activity with budget allocation."[21] Several other committees, including banking, merchant marine, and interior, endorsed the concept of a credit budget, but called for higher limits on the programs within their jurisdiction.[22] Small business, agriculture, and education and labor objected to proposed program limits and argued that for certain programs annual limits would reduce necessary flexibility in program implementation.[23]

The House and Senate budget committees, which expressed disappointment in the modest scope of the Carter proposal, were thus confronted with objections from other committees that the Carter credit budget went too far.[24] There was also considerable uncertainty among budget committee members over how much latitude they enjoyed under the 1974 budget act. The result was the inclusion of credit budget totals in the first and second concurrent budget resolutions for fiscal 1981 but no agreement on enforcement procedures.

Committee Proposals

The House Budget Committee, which proposed credit budget aggregates only slightly below those recommended by President Carter, was less concerned with the totals than with expanding appropriations bill limitations (see Table

Table 5.4 House Budget Committee Credit Budget Recommendations, Fiscal Year 1981 (in billions of dollars)

	President's January Budget	Budget Committee Recommendation
Credit Budget Aggregates		
New direct loan obligations	60.7	60.6
New primary loan guarantee commitments	81.4	79.5
Total, credit budget	142.1	140.2
Proposed Limitations		
Direct loan obligations	27.2	60.6
Loan guarantee commitments (primary)	32.5	79.5
Loan guarantee commitments, secondary, and guarantees of direct loans	—	78.9
Total, proposed limitations	59.7	219.1

Source: House Committee on the Budget, *Report No. 96-857, First Concurrent Resolution on the Budget—Fiscal Year 1981* (Washington, D.C.: Government Printing Office, 1980), p. 20.

5.4). It recommended that annual appropriations ceilings be extended to all new direct loan obligations and loan guarantee commitments. It also called for limits on secondary loan guarantees and guarantees of direct loans by other agencies. As the committee's report noted, "This would allow coverage of financing activities of the Federal Financing Bank."[25] It also meant the appropriations committees would be dealing with approximately $220 billion rather than $60 billion in program limitations.

The Senate Budget Committee, which had established a special subcommittee to review the Carter proposals, came up with a different mix on credit totals—more than $4 billion less than the president's plan on loan guarantees but more than $3 billion in additional direct loans. The committee also adopted a different enforcement proposal from that proposed by its House counterpart. First, it recommended that the budget resolution contain a sense-of-Congress provision directing the president and the Congress to enforce, through the appropriations process, specified limits for on-budget lending, off-budget lending, and new primary loan guarantee commitments. Second, it proposed that all new credit legislation be subject to appropriation limitations: "It shall not be in order in the House or Senate to consider any bill, resolution, or amendment authorizing new direct loans or new loan guarantees unless that bill, resolution, or amendment also provides that the authority to make or guarantee such loans shall be effective only to such extent or in such amounts as are contained in appropriation Acts." [26]

Budget Resolutions

The first concurrent budget resolution for fiscal 1981 was adopted on 12 June, nearly a month after the statutory deadline and only after several weeks of conference bargaining that saw the House reject the initial conference compromise. The conference conflict, however, had little to do with the credit budget; rather, it reflected the debate over defense–social welfare priorities that had divided the House and Senate for several years. The conference agreed to the House Budget Committee's figure for loan guarantees and to the Senate committee's figure for direct loans, both of which represented the higher program levels. With respect to enforcement, the conferees agreed to the sense-of-Congress provision that the Senate Budget Committee had proposed, but it dropped the procedural restriction governing new credit legislation as well as the House committee's plan to expand appropriations limits to all fiscal 1981 credit activity.

What the credit budget language amounted to, therefore, was a set of informal guidelines. The potential coverage was somewhat broader than the Carter credit system, since there were ceilings for on-budget and off-budget lending that would permit appropriations limits on FFB activity, but given the potential opposition from authorizing committees, it was unlikely that the appropriations committees would be willing to go that far.

By the time Congress adopted its second fiscal 1981 budget resolution— some two months after the statutory deadline and, more important, after the 1980 presidential election—spending control problems had become so severe that credit was largely ignored. The budget committees were able to include credit aggregates for direct loans and loan guarantees in the resolution, and the loan guarantee totals were further divided between primary and secondary guarantees. The Senate Budget Committee's attempt to distribute the credit aggregates among the functional budget categories (as was done with outlays and budget authority) and to include this allocation in the language of the resolution was unsuccessful.

Appropriation Limits

The appropriations committees, which were able to clear only three appropriations bills by the beginning of fiscal 1981, lost much of their initial enthusiasm for taking on credit programs. They did adopt program limitations in some cases, but these did not go as far as President Carter had recommended and were even further removed from the limits assumed in the first congressional budget resolution for fiscal 1981.[27] In the second fiscal 1981 budget resolution, the budget committees were forced to raise the direct loan target by almost $10 billion over the first resolution, and the recommended limit on new loan guarantee commitments was increased by more than $3 billion.

Moreover, even where annual program limits were included in appropriation language, their effects were sometimes uncertain. The appropriation bill for Housing and Urban Development specified $885 million in gross commitments as the fiscal 1981 ceiling for the Housing for the Elderly or Handicapped Fund, but provided that an additional $65 million could be used from prior-year commitments that had been canceled.[28] A similar provision was included for the housing rehabilitation loan fund.[29] For other housing programs, such as low-rent public housing, the statute simply provided that direct loans and loan guarantees "are authorized in such amounts as may be necessary."[30]

For the other major credit category, agriculture, limits were similarly elastic. The FmHA credit programs were set at extremely generous levels, even though almost $300 million in appropriated funds was required to cover losses in the Agricultural Credit and Rural Insurance Funds.[31] A $3.3 billion reimbursement for the Commodity Credit Corporation's prior-year losses was also required, but no fiscal year limitation was established for the CCC's current operations.[32] For the Rural Electrification Administration and Rural Telephone Bank, program levels were included in the agriculture appropriation bill, but as in previous years these were to insure that program activity was not reduced, and the appropriation committees refused to include any limits for loan guarantees.[33] The committees also mandated continued high levels of FFB purchases of agricultural loans, specifying that FmHA sales of certificates of beneficial ownership "shall be not less than 75 per centum of the value of the loans closed during the fiscal year."[34] This did not portend well for the sense-of-Congress limits on off-budget lending contained in the first and second budget resolutions.

What started as a modest proposal in the executive branch became even more modest as Congress wrestled with the jurisdictional and programmatic implications of a credit control system. The budget committees achieved a victory of sorts by including credit targets in the fiscal 1981 budget resolutions, but the effect was largely symbolic. While interested in jurisdictional expansion, the appropriations committees were unwilling to mount any serious challenge to large, popular credit programs. Indeed, the incentives for Congress to support such a challenge were minimal, so long as the economic implications of credit policy were uncertain and the budgetary effects complex.

The Credit Budget Record

The impact on federal credit during fiscal 1981 was mixed. Outstanding federal credit (direct loans and loan guarantees) increased by about 7 percent over fiscal 1980 levels, but this was considerably less than the 12 percent growth rate originally projected (see Table 5.5). Compared to the spending budget, where the outlay growth rate was double initial estimates, the credit budget did fairly well.

The overall record on credit, however, covered up a number of serious estimating errors. Using the original Carter budget, for example, there were substantial underestimates for new direct loan obligations, both on-budget and off-budget. On-budget direct loans were more than $5 billion higher than estimated, while off-budget obligations were more than $6 billion higher (see Table 5.6). As a result, net outlays attributable to direct lending came to $26 billion, although only $5 billion of this was carried on budget. For individual programs, estimating errors were substantial as well—FFB activity was $7 billion over estimates, FmHA programs were $4 billion over, while the Export-Import Bank was $1.5 billion under administration projections.

For loan guarantees, the fiscal 1981 results were more positive. Actual commitments were almost $5 billion under the $81.4 billion initial estimate. As shown in Table 5.7, however, this was the result of greatly decreased demand for housing loans. No appropriation limit had been requested for general housing guarantees precisely in order to encourage program activity. By comparison, guarantees for student loans and other education credit programs were $7.5 billion over estimates.

The credit budget did not provide, therefore, very precise control. It did not constrain program activity, even where appropriation limits were implemented. And it did not achieve consistent treatment of programs. Some were still governed by demand, others by appropriations language, and still others by administrative discretion.

The Carter administration's fiscal 1982 credit budget, moreover, did not propose any major changes in the credit budget control system or coverage. It projected a substantial increase in outstanding credit—some $85 billion over the prior-year estimates—and called for appropriations limits on only 29 percent of new transactions compared to 40 percent the previous year.[35]

The fiscal 1982 budget implicitly acknowledged the inadequacy of the credit budget initiative. It called for the establishment of a "panel of outstanding financial and budget experts" to examine the state of federal credit policy.[36] President Carter's budget message proposed that the commission be given a broad responsibility: "[It] should consider the treatment of credit ac-

Table 5.5 Federal Credit Outstanding, Fiscal Years 1979–1981 (in billions of dollars)

	Fiscal Year 1979	Fiscal Year 1980	Fiscal Year 1981 Estimate	Fiscal Year 1981 Actual
Direct Loans				
On-budget	83.0	91.7	88.5	91.3
Off-budget	57.5	72.3	90.8	93.7
Primary Guaranteed Loans	264.6	298.5	339.5	309.0
Totals	405.1	462.5	518.8	494.0

Source: *Special Analysis, Federal Credit Programs, Budget of the United States Government*, Fiscal Years 1981–83.

Table 5.6 Direct Loans—Credit Budget versus Program Activity, Fiscal Year 1981 (in billions of dollars)

	Original Carter Budget	Fiscal 1981 Actual
New Direct Loan Obligations		
On-budget agencies	35.4	40.8
Off-budget agencies	25.2	31.5
Totals	60.6	72.4
Net Outlays		
On-budget agencies	−0.6	5.1
Off-budget agencies	16.6	20.9
Totals	16.0	26.0

Source: Direct loan obligations figures are from *Budget of the United States Government, Fiscal Year 1981* (Washington, D.C.: Government Printing Office, 1980), p. 596, and *Budget of the United States Government, Fiscal Year 1983* (Washington, D.C.: Government Printing Office, 1982), p. 9-44. Net outlay figures are from *Special Analysis F, Federal Credit Programs*, Fiscal Years 1981, 1983.

tivities in the budget, the adequacy of program administration, uniform rules and procedures for federal credit programs, the role of the Federal Financing Bank, and the relationship of tax-exempt financing to overall credit and tax policies." [37] And in order to lend some urgency to this recommendation, President Carter reported that a two-year study of federal credit administration had

Table 5.7 Loan Guarantees—Credit Budget versus Program Activity, Fiscal Year 1981 (in billions of dollars)

Department or Agency	Original Carter Budget	Fiscal 1981 Actual
Agriculture	21.4	22.6
Commerce	3.2	3.5
Education	2.2	9.7
Housing and Urban Development	102.1	85.3
Veterans Administration	10.3	11.7
Export-Import Bank	8.9	7.4
Small Business Administration	5.7	3.6
All other	6.4	8.9
Sub-total	160.2	152.7
Less secondary guaranteed loans	−53.1	−44.1
Less guaranteed loans held as direct loans	−25.8	−32.1
Total, primary guaranteed loans	81.4	76.5

Source: *Budget of the United States Government, Fiscal Year 1981* (Washington, D.C.: Government Printing Office, 1980), p. 597; *Budget of the United States Government, Fiscal Year 1983* (Washington, D.C.: Government Printing Office, 1982), p. 9-45.

found $25 billion in delinquent or defaulted loans out of $175 billion in accounts and loans receivable.[38] The electoral results of November 1980, however, had pretty much insured that the Carter administration's latest thoughts on budget control would not command much attention.

The Ford and Carter Presidencies

Over a five-year period spanning the Ford and Carter presidencies, credit control reforms began to receive increased attention in the executive branch and Congress. The increased attention, however, did not result in enforceable credit budgets or in more accurate budget accounting. President Ford's proposals to eliminate off-budget lending and transfer all credit activity on budget were never seriously considered by Congress. President Carter's credit budget was a modest improvement that increased the visibility of credit programs and forced Congress to deal with credit totals. Its very modesty, however, precluded serious efforts in Congress to enforce credit totals.

The possibility for effective enforcement was further reduced by the inability of both branches to control the spending budget. As spending growth rates remained high and deficits grew, there were obvious incentives to exploit rather than eliminate off-budget credit routes. Thus, credit reform was continually subordinated to short-term budgetary considerations. In retrospect, the Ford administration's straightforward proposal to eliminate the favored status of off-budget agencies would have solved a problem that the more elaborate credit budget and control system simply perpetuated—the unequal treatment of spending and credit.

It is also worth noting that, despite the increased information available about credit programs, crucial issues were largely ignored. The economic effects, subsidies, and risks associated with credit programs remained largely unexplored in presidential budgets and congressional debates. The credit budget did not illuminate the true costs of credit programs, and this allowed the executive branch and Congress to continue to treat certain types of credit as cost-free.

Chapter 6

The Reagan Initiatives

Shortly after taking office, President Reagan unveiled an ambitious program designed to alter the size and shape of the federal budget. Considerable attention and controversy have since been directed toward his spending and tax proposals. The administration has also made, however, less publicized initiatives aimed at arresting and eventually reversing the expansion of federal credit activity. Many direct loans and loan guarantee programs have been slated for reduction, some for termination, and only a very few for continued support. The administration's credit policy proposals, then, are considerably more stringent than its spending recommendations, which have allowed for modest rates of growth.

In defending its reductions in the size and scope of the credit budget, the administration has advanced two primary justifications. The first applies to programs, such as guaranteed student loans and general housing programs, for which eligibility criteria have been criticized as too broad and the resulting subsidies as inappropriate. The second relates to credit programs "that were designed to promote economic development," but, in the administration's view, "[have] had either little or no measurable results or [have] exacerbated existing problems by interfering with the efficiency of private financial markets." [1]

Under the Reagan program, credit restraint is to be imposed through policy changes, primarily statutory limits on program levels, and through administration actions to reduce lending levels. Both these methods have encountered difficulty in Congress. There were numerous credit program cuts in 1981, but subsequent program-by-program reductions have generally encountered stiff opposition in Congress. Unilateral administrative reductions have been attacked in Congress as analogous to spending impoundments and countered through mandatory program levels. Major program cuts, at least on the scale proposed by the administration, have not been achieved.

There have been, however, some procedural advances in congressional decision making on credit matters. Various enforcement provisions for the credit budget have been included on a temporary basis in the fiscal 1983 and 1984 congressional budget resolutions, and legislation has been proposed that would make the credit budget a permanent part of the congressional budget process.

Proposals have also been introduced that would change the budgetary treatment of the Federal Financing Bank's operations, improve program reporting to Congress, and require standardized treatment by the various agencies of defaults and program costs.

These initiatives reflect the growing concern among members of Congress over the scope and effects of federal credit intervention, and indeed, looking at recent credit budget totals, it appears that the growth of federal credit activity has been curbed. This progress is largely illusory, however, reflecting changing economic conditions rather than deliberate political choices. Effective credit control is linked to policy and procedural issues that have yet to be resolved. The Reagan credit program has highlighted the policy issues and, in so doing, has forced Congress to confront the political costs of reduced credit intervention. Whether Congress will respond, and how, is uncertain, but prospects for immediate resolution are not especially promising.

Spending and Credit Totals

The principal feature of the credit budget is its limitation, or ceiling, on aggregate credit activity—new direct loan obligations and new loan guarantee commitments. In assessing budgetary control, the stringency and accuracy of aggregate limits is obviously important, for credit just as for direct spending. Based on these criteria, the credit budget has clearly outperformed the spending budget over the past several years.

The contrasts are evident in executive branch budget proposals and congressional budget resolutions. The Reagan administration, for example, has proposed relatively low percentage increases in direct spending for fiscal years 1981–84, and similar rates of growth have been projected through the mid-1980s (see Table 6.1). The average annual growth rate of approximately 6 percent contained in Reagan spending proposals is about half the actual rate for the 1970s and represents estimated real growth of about 15 percent for the fiscal 1981–86 period.[2] Congressional budget resolutions are roughly comparable in total outlays.[3] Despite this agreement on aggregate spending policy, actual spending has run substantially above both administration and congressional estimates during fiscal years 1982 and 1983, and there is a reasonable likelihood this pattern will continue in the fiscal 1984 and out-year budgets. As a result of these spending underestimates, and revenue overestimates, unified budget deficits have been far above planned levels.

Presidential and congressional credit budgets differ to a greater extent than direct spending budgets. Congressional credit budget totals are, on average,

Table 6.1 Reagan Administration and Congressional Spending and Credit Budget Aggregates, Fiscal Years 1981–1986 (in billions of dollars)

	Original Reagan Budget	First Concurrent Budget Resolution	Actual
Fiscal Year 1981[a]			
Total outlays	$655.2	$613.6	$657.2
Total credit[b]	140.2	143.5	133.7
Fiscal Year 1982			
Total outlays	695.3	695.45	728.4
Total credit	129.2	154.1[c]	108.7
Fiscal Year 1983			
Total outlays	757.6	769.8	805.2 (est.)
Total credit	147.3	161.6	158.7 (est.)
Fiscal Year 1984[d]			
Total outlays	848.5	858.9	NA
Total credit	144.2	149.6	
Fiscal Year 1985[e]			
Total outlays	918.5	911.6	NA
Total credit	143.4	154.4	
Fiscal Year 1986			
Total outlays	989.6	966.6	NA
Total credit	142.1	154.55	

Source: Congressional Budget Office, *Federal Credit Activities*, Fiscal Years 1982–83; House and Senate Budget Committees, *First Concurrent Budget Resolution*, Fiscal Years 1983–84; *Special Analysis, Federal Credit Programs, Budget of the United States Government*, Fiscal Years 1982–84.

a. The original Reagan budget for fiscal 1981 was part of the fiscal year 1982 budget revisions submitted to Congress in March 1981.

b. Totals are not adjusted for repurchases of loan assets for all years shown.

c. Adjusted to show full principal of guaranteed loans for comparability with administration recommendations.

d. Congressional outlay and credit budget totals for fiscal years 1984–86 include reserve funds contained in sec. 2(a) of the first concurrent budget resolution for fiscal 1984.

e. Figures for fiscal years 1985–86 are out-year estimates contained in the administration and congressional budgets for fiscal 1984.

about 8 percent higher than those proposed by the Reagan administration. Neither side, however, projects much growth in credit activity, at least through the mid-1980s. There are year-to-year variations in aggregate new lending, but in real terms the fiscal 1986 projections are about the same as fiscal 1981 lending.

Recent credit budgets, then, have been more stringent than spending budgets, and this disparity should continue at least for the next few years. In addition, the credit budget aggregates have not been breached. As against massive spending underestimates for fiscal years 1981–83, there is a net credit shortfall of $15–60 billion, depending upon whether one uses the executive branch or congressional credit budget totals. Finally, and again in sharp contrast to spending figures, the out-year levels currently projected for credit activity are likely fully to accommodate credit program activity.[4]

It is necessary, however, to distinguish between the effects of deliberate policy reductions and unanticipated economic conditions in analyzing the shortfalls in credit activity. As with spending estimates, credit program estimates are subject to a good deal of uncertainty, and it is usually difficult to make precise judgments about the sources of error for either. Nevertheless, there is evidence that much of the "control" in recent credit budgets can be attributed to economic factors rather than to policy reductions.

Participation Rates and Credit Demand

One indication of this is the stability of federal participation rates, despite the drop in new federal credit. The rate for 1982 was 21.4 percent, compared to 20.2 percent in 1981 and 21.8 percent in 1980.[5] Total funds advanced in credit markets increased by over $60 billion between 1980 and 1981, but there was a decline of almost $20 billion between 1981 and 1982. The sharp reduction in the federal credit budget for fiscal 1982, therefore, was part of an overall drop in domestic credit.

In addition, much of the volatility in the credit budget has been in demand-based programs rather than discretionary lending. Loan guarantees to support housing declined sharply during the fiscal 1981–82 period, accounting for much of the $25 billion reduction in total new credit. The estimated $50 billion increase for fiscal 1983 likewise reflects an anticipated major shift in demand for housing credit.

A recent analysis of the relative effects of policy reductions and economic conditions on credit budget totals suggests rather substantial differentials.[6] For fiscal years 1981–83 the estimated impact of economic factors is two to four times greater than that of policy reductions for direct loan programs. For guaranteed loans the corresponding estimates are roughly eight to one for 1981–82 program level changes and nearly ten to one for 1982–83 changes.

Agency and Program Estimates

Within the credit budget totals, there have also been substantial errors— underestimates and overestimates—for individual programs. As shown in Table 6.2, the Reagan credit budget for fiscal 1982 was substantially off the mark for a number of direct and guaranteed lending programs. Agricultural lending ran well above estimates, particularly for new direct loan obligations. Export-Import Bank lending declined by over $3 billion compared to 1980 direct loan and loan guarantee totals, while administration estimates showed an increase in lending activity. The reduction in Small Business Administration lending was much greater than anticipated. And, of course, loan guarantees for housing were overestimated by almost $50 billion. The very large overestimate for new loan guarantee commitments, in fact, covered up what would otherwise have been a significant underestimate for new direct loan obligations.

Policy Reductions

This does not mean that no policy reductions have been implemented. The Omnibus Budget Reconciliation Act of 1981, which the Reagan administration sponsored, reduced program levels, eligibility, and subsidies in a variety of credit programs. Among these were selected FmHA, Small Business Administration, and Export-Import Bank lending activities, along with guaranteed student loans and Rural Electrification Administration direct loans. Congress accepted the administration's recommendation to make the National Consumer Cooperative Bank a private enterprise, but it rejected termination proposals for several large programs, including the Government National Mortgage Association (GNMA) tandem (or special assistance) plan and college housing loans.

By the fall of 1981, however, the Reagan administration was recommending additional spending and credit cuts. On 24 September 1981, President Reagan announced that a new round of budget reductions was needed to control the fiscal 1982 deficit and the accompanying federal credit demands on capital markets. Along with approximately $13 billion in direct spending cuts, the president announced that $20 billion in loan guarantees would also be eliminated: "These guarantees are not funds that the government spends

**Table 6.2 Estimated and Actual Changes in New Lending, by Agency,
Fiscal Years 1980–1982
(in billions of dollars)**

	Estimated Change 1980–82 President's Budget	Actual Change 1980–82
New Direct Loan Obligations		
Funds appropriated to the President (International security and development assistance)	+1.4	+0.1
Agriculture	−6.9[a]	+6.2
Housing and Urban Development	—	−1.0
Veterans Administration	—	+0.3
Export-Import Bank	—	−0.9
National Credit Union Administration	+3.4	−0.2
Small Business Administration	−0.8	−1.1
Rural Electrification Administration	−0.5	+0.1
All other agencies	−1.2	+2.6
Total direct loan obligations	−4.5	+6.1
New Loan Guarantee Commitments		
Funds appropriated to the President (International security and development assistance)	+1.0	+1.5
Agriculture	−5.6	+0.3
Education	+0.4	+1.1
Housing and Urban Development	+7.5	−41.0
Veterans Administration	+1.1	−0.3
Export-Import Bank	+0.2	−2.2
Small Business Administration	−0.4	−2.7
All other	+6.0	+3.1
Total new loan guarantee commitments	+10.2	−40.2

Source: *Fiscal Year 1982 Budget Revisions* (Washington, D.C.: Government Printing Office, March 1981), pp. 130–31; *Budget of the United States Government, Fiscal Year 1984* (Washington, D.C.: Government Printing Office, 1983), pp. 9-36–9-37.

a. The original table from which this is calculated shows a reduction of $8.2 billion. The corrected figure is $6.9 billion, representing an adjustment of $1.3 billion for agricultural credit insurance fund direct loan obligations.

directly. They're funds that are loaned in the private market and insured by government at subsidized rates. Federal loan guarantees have become a form of back door, uncontrolled borrowing that prevent many small businesses that aren't subsidized from obtaining financing of their own. They are also a major factor in driving up interest rates." [7]

On 5 November the White House released the specifics of the president's plan. Total reductions of $20.3 billion in loan guarantee commitments were included, covering fourteen programs administered by nine departments and agencies. Hardest hit were four programs—GNMA mortgage-backed securities, the Rural Electrification and Telephone Revolving Fund, Export-Import Bank guarantees, and Small Business Administration credit assistance—that accounted for 95 percent of the proposed cuts. [8]

Congress was not at all enthusiatic about either the spending or credit proposals. The resulting spending impasse forced the use of three continuing resolutions to finance government operations during the first quarter of fiscal 1982. Even with a presidential veto of the initial version of the second continuing resolution—a veto that was sustained—the spending levels finally enacted were above those proposed by the administration.

With Congress unwilling to follow the president's lead on a second round of major budget cuts, there were intimations from the executive branch that impoundments might be used to limit fiscal 1982 spending, at least until final appropriations were enacted. The first continuing resolution for fiscal 1982, which funded all appropriated activities, established program spending levels at "a rate for operations not exceeding" that contained in the resolution. [9] It was therefore unclear whether the resolution language merely set a ceiling (which was the view of the Senate Appropriations Committee leadership) or mandated spending at specified levels, as House Appropriations Committee Democrats insisted.

In any case, the Office of Management and Budget ordered executive agencies to spend at the level of the president's September budget requests in those instances where the continuing resolution contained higher spending levels. These instructions were undertaken in compliance with the impoundment control provisions of the 1974 budget act, which allowed the president to defer spending within a fiscal year subject to either a House or Senate veto of a formal deferral request. Five separate deferral messages, containing over two hundred deferrals and totaling $2.7 billion in outlays, were sent to Congress during October and November of 1981. Since none of these requests was disapproved, the president was able to hold spending to his September budget levels for the period covered by the continuing resolution.

While Congress could reject spending deferrals, thereby requiring immediate commitments of funds at higher levels, it did not have a direct means of countering impoundments applied to loan guarantee programs. Loan guarantees are not considered budget authority under the 1974 act and do not come under the Title 10 impoundment checks. In an effort to prevent the administration from unilaterally imposing ceilings on the various loan guarantee programs for which the president had announced reductions, "anti-impoundment" language was added to the third continuing resolution for fiscal 1982, which was enacted 15 December 1981. Section 136 of the resolution (the Levin amendment, introduced by Senator Carl Levin [D-Mich.]) prohibited discretionary cuts in loan guarantee programs:

> Notwithstanding any other provision of this joint resolution, subject only to the absence of qualified applicants, and within the limits of funds and authority available, the head of each department and agency for which authority to enter into commitments to guarantee or insure is provided for . . . shall enter into commitments to guarantee or insure in the full amounts provided for in this joint resolution or other applicable law.[10]

A similar provision was added to the first continuing appropriations bill for fiscal 1983. Section 145 of PL 97-276 provided that, in addition to demand limits, program levels could also be reduced by limitations contained in appropriations acts. Several authorizing statutes enacted during 1982 also included mandatory language to protect congressionally established levels for loan guarantees.[11] Senator Levin has since introduced legislation that would treat loan guarantees in the same manner as budget authority for purposes of Title 10 impoundment controls.[12]

In response to the adoption of the Levin amendment, the Reagan administration requested additional appropriations and, in some cases, authorization limitations to reduce loan guarantee program levels during fiscal 1982. The largest request was for a $20 billion reduction affecting GNMA mortgage-backed securities purchases, but major reductions were proposed as well for the Rural Electrification Administration and Small Business Administration. In each instance, Congress either refused to enact a limit or established one considerably higher than the president's request.[13]

President Reagan's proposals for reductions in spending and credit for fiscal 1982 met a similar fate in Congress. After considerable controversy, an initial round of program reductions was enacted, using the omnibus reconciliation procedure. While substantial, these reductions were not sufficient to meet the administration's targets for spending or credit, and the president proposed another round of cuts. These encountered much stiffer resistance in

Congress and were only partially achieved. During 1982 and, especially, 1983, congressional resistance hardened still further, essentially precluding dramatic spending or credit reductions.

The spending and credit budgets diverged sharply, however, in actual program levels. While spending was boosted by the 1981–82 recession, credit demand plummeted. After all the controversy regarding loan guarantees, commitments dropped well under even administration estimates. In effect, the actual spending totals for fiscal 1982 and, to a lesser extent, 1983 probably understate the extent of policy reductions and the impact of President Reagan's program. The credit totals, by contrast, substantially overstate his success in persuading Congress to curtail federal credit programs.

The Reagan Policy Agenda

Most of the major confrontations over federal credit programs have yet to be fought, much less decided. Both the Reagan administration and Congress expected a major increase in the credit budget—as much as 50 percent over fiscal 1982 levels—during fiscal 1983. Virtually all of this was tied to economic recovery, notably a revived housing market and increased demand for mortgage credit, rather than to policy changes. The credit budget totals for fiscal 1983, especially in Congress's case, were designed to accommodate this increased credit demand, not to restrain federal credit activity.

President Reagan's fiscal 1984 budget, however, is much more ambitious. It calls for permanent, long-term reductions in almost every major credit program and in overall federal credit intervention. Included are proposals for restrictive appropriations limits, reduced eligibility and subsidies, and, in a few cases, program terminations.

Since for the first time the components of the credit budget have been projected for a five-year period, the long-term impact of the administration's policy agenda is clear. According to the Congressional Budget Office, President Reagan's proposals amount to "a reduction of almost $150 billion from what would otherwise occur under current policies." [14] Direct lending would be reduced by about 25 percent and primary guaranteed loans by about 15 percent compared to lending levels that would result under current policies. [15]

The proposed cuts extend to virtually all programs. The only increases contained in the fiscal 1984 recommendations are short-term boosts in Export-Import Bank guarantees and foreign military sales credits. Even these programs, however, would be held below the current policy baseline over the entire fiscal 1984–88 period.

Budget estimates are, of course, subject to considerable uncertainty, and long-range projections are especially unreliable. The presidential estimates and baseline comparisons are therefore tenuous as far as numerically precise program level changes are concerned. Those estimates, however, are tied to legislative changes that definitely would reduce program levels, if perhaps not by the exact amount that baseline comparisons suggest.

Program Reductions

As shown in Table 6.3, the bulk of the Reagan credit reductions are concentrated in a relatively small number of programs. Some of the largest cuts are justified by reasons of reduced demand. The projected FHA program levels, for example, "reflect an expanding role for private mortgage insurers." [16] REA program levels are based on "lower demand in the electric market, reducing the need for assistance to REA borrowers." [17]

The attempt to cast these and similar reductions in the context of changing demand is not likely to persuade many in Congress. The reductions are in fact significant policy changes that would further the administration's goal of curtailing federal credit allocation. The program levels in the president's budget are not only considerably below those Congress has established in the past but comparable to those Congress deliberately rejected during the first two years of the Reagan presidency.

Other program reductions will also require congressional concurrence of various types (see Table 6.4), and here again the prospects are not promising. For example, one of the largest and most heavily subsidized direct loan programs—the FmHA's low-income housing loans—funded ninety thousand rural housing units at a program level of $3.4 billion in fiscal 1983.[18] The Reagan credit budget calls for terminating new loans in fiscal 1984 and establishing a block grant to the states to support rural housing. Terminations and major reductions have been proposed for Small Business Administration direct loans and loan guarantees, and the administration wants to end the GNMA tandem plan that subsidizes FHA and VA loans at below market interest rates. Eligibility for guaranteed student loans would be reduced by requiring a needs analysis for all potential borrowers, a step the Congressional Budget Office estimates would affect seven hundred thousand students.[19] Subsidies would also be reduced through higher origination fees.

In another controversial move, the Reagan credit budget proposes that the budgetary treatment of FmHA loan asset sales be changed. It would require that loan assets sold to the FFB by the rural housing insurance fund be treated as agency borrowing, not as offsets to current outlays. In addition, the FFB's

Table 6.3 Reagan Administration Proposed Reductions in Credit Programs, Fiscal Years 1984–1988 (in billions of dollars)

	Proposed Net Changes from Congressional Budget Office Baseline, FY 1984–88
Direct Loan Obligations	
Foreign military credit sales	−0.3
Export-Import Bank	−6.0
Rural housing insurance fund	−19.6
Rural Electrification Administration	−14.3
Commodity Credit Corporation	−2.8
GNMA special assistance functions fund	−2.9
Agriculture credit insurance fund	−5.3
SBA disaster loan fund	−2.8
Other	−8.8
Total direct loan obligations	−62.8
Primary Loan Guarantees	
Export-Import Bank	−1.4
Rural Electrification Administration	(−12.2)[a]
SBA business loan and investment fund	−9.7
FHA mortgage insurance	−63.5
GNMA mortgage-backed securities	(−96.8)[a]
Guaranteed student loans	−4.9
Other	−2.9
Total primary loan guarantees	−82.4

Source: Congressional Budget Office, *An Analysis of the President's Credit Budget for Fiscal Year 1984* (Washington, D.C.: Congressional Budget Office, March 1983), pp. 19–20.
   a. These are intragovernmental transactions that are not included in the totals.

portfolio of more than $25 billion in rural housing insurance fund loan assets would be converted to agency debt. The result of this change would ultimately be to reduce FFB off-budget outlays and to increase the on-budget outlays of the rural housing insurance fund. Whether the fund could then compete effectively for budgetary resources with on-budget programs is precisely the question that makes this apparently technical issue politically controversial.

Finally, unlike its predecessors, the Reagan administration has challenged the status of government-sponsored enterprises. It has strongly opposed, for example, legislation that would broaden the secondary market activities of the Federal National Mortgage Association and a recapitalization plan that would expand the operations of the Federal Home Loan Mortgage Corporation. In each case, administration spokesmen have argued against any changes that are not linked to reduced ties with the government.

Moreover, OMB has developed proposals to coordinate the full "privatization" of all government-sponsored enterprises. As explained by Lawrence A. Kudlow, former associate director for economics and planning at OMB, privatization is an integral part of the Reagan administration's long-term plan for reducing federal credit intervention:

> The President believes that the economy is best served by strong private financial intermediaries; and any exception seriously erodes the Administration's general policy of avoiding special relief measures for particular industries or economic sectors. With this in mind, it is antici-

Table 6.4 Action Required to Effect Major Program Reductions, Reagan Fiscal 1984 Credit Budget

Program/Agency	Legislative Action Required
Commodity Credit Corporation	None (Implemented payment-in-kind program)
FmHA Agricultural Credit Insurance Fund	Appropriation Limits
FmHA Rural Housing Insurance Fund	Authorization/Appropriation (Replaced with block grant)
Federal Housing Administration	Authorization/Appropriation Limits
GNMA Tandem (Special Assistance) Plan	Authorization (Termination)
GNMA Mortgage-Backed Securities	Appropriation Limits
Guaranteed Student Loans	Authorization (Eligibility and subsidy restrictions)
Maritime Administration Ship Financing Fund	Appropriation Limits
SBA Business Loan and Investment Fund	Authorization (Termination)
SBA Disaster Loans	Appropriation Limits
SBA Pollution Control Equipment Guarantees	Appropriation Limits

pated that a number of the special competitive advantages now accorded to government-sponsored enterprises will be gradually phased out, encouraging each organization to compete equally with other private, unsubsidized financial intermediaries.[20]

Privatization would require, of course, numerous statutory changes, as well as financial regulatory initiatives. A comprehensive plan is scheduled for submission to Congress during fiscal 1984.

The Reagan agenda, then, is the first comprehensive effort to redefine federal credit policy. Its implementation would reverse the long-term growth of federal credit intervention. It would greatly reduce, for example, federal lending as a percentage of gross national product. From 1973 through 1982, credit activity tripled while GNP doubled.[21] Under current policy, credit activity will decline only slightly as a percentage of GNP through 1988. Under the Reagan credit budget, the decline would be much sharper, bringing federal credit down to less than 3 percent of GNP by 1988, about 1 percentage point under the current policy level.[22] The long-term plan for credit resembles that for spending—to reduce the percentage of GNP by keeping government growth under economic growth. But the proportionate reduction for credit is considerably greater than that for spending.[23]

There are, however, obstacles to enactment of the Reagan credit agenda. One of the most serious is the lack of budgetary incentives that would lead Congress to cooperate. As shown in Table 6.5, the impact of the president's proposed credit budget changes on on-budget outlays is minimal. The off-budget estimated savings are twice as large. Of particular importance, only $300 million in on-budget savings would be realized during fiscal 1984, when Congress would be expected to make painful policy reductions during a pre-election period. Not until fiscal 1987 would substantial on-budget savings be realized, and even these would hardly be noticed in a budget of perhaps $1.1 trillion. In addition, some of the proposed policy reductions—such as the cutbacks in GNMA mortgage-backed securities and FHA mortgage assistance—would actually increase outlays, since these programs make money.[24]

The impact of the Reagan credit program on outlays and deficits, then, hardly appears proportionate to the political costs of program reductions that Congress is being asked to make. Moreover, that impact is scattered among a number of different programs. In the absence of sufficient budgetary incentives, the rationale for reversing federal credit intervention necessarily rests on general economic considerations, and here the administration cannot produce clear-cut evidence. There is no consensus at the present time on the market effects of federal credit activity, although there is certainly a good deal of

Table 6.5 Estimated Outlay Impact of Reagan Credit Budget Proposals, Fiscal Years 1984–1988 (in billions of dollars)

	Fiscal Year					Cumulative Five-Year Changes
	1984	1985	1986	1987	1988	
On-Budget Outlay Changes						
Export-Import Bank	a	−0.3	−0.5	−0.7	−0.8	−2.3
Foreign Military Sales Credit	−0.1	−0.3	−0.3	−0.4	−0.4	−1.5
Agriculture Credit Insurance Fund (FmHA)	−0.2	−0.1	−0.1	−0.1	−0.2	−0.7
Rural Housing Insurance Fund (FmHA)	0.3	−0.6	−0.7	−1.2	−1.5	−3.7
GNMA Mortgage-Backed Securities	a	a	a	a	a	a
GNMA Special Assistance Functions Fund	—	a	−0.1	−1.5	−1.7	−3.3
FHA Mortgage Assistance	—	0.3	0.4	0.4	0.5	1.6
SBA Disaster Loan Fund	−0.3	−0.5	−0.4	−0.4	−0.4	−2.0
Guaranteed Student Loans	a	−0.1	−0.2	−0.2	−0.2	−0.7
Other	NA	NA	NA	NA	NA	NA
Subtotal	−0.3	−1.6	−1.9	−4.1	−4.7	−12.6
Off-Budget Outlay Changes						
Foreign Military Sales Credit	0.4	0.3	0.2	0.1	−0.1	0.9
Rural Electrification Administration	−0.1	−0.9	−1.5	−2.1	−2.5	−7.1
Agriculture Credit Insurance Fund (FmHA)	−0.6	−0.8	−1.1	−1.3	−1.5	−5.3
Rural Housing Insurance Fund (FmHA)	−2.4	−2.5	−2.6	−2.7	−2.8	−13.0
SBA Business Loan Investment Fund	−0.1	−0.1	−0.2	−0.2	−0.2	−0.8
Subtotal	−2.8	−4.0	−5.2	−6.2	−7.1	−25.2
Combined On-Budget/Off-Budget Outlay Impact	−3.1	−5.6	−7.0	−10.2	−11.7	−37.6

Source: Congressional Budget Office, *An Analysis of the President's Credit Budget for Fiscal Year 1984* (Washington, D.C.: Congressional Budget Office, March 1983), p. 25.

a. Less than $50 million

concern. And it is difficult in any event to use macroeconomic arguments against federal credit programs while enormous budget deficits are directly affecting credit availability. If the goals for spending growth and deficits that the Reagan administration originally submitted had been achieved over the past two years, it is possible that the prospects for credit reductions might be better. The unprecedented amounts of spending and deficit underestimates, however, have made it much more difficult to interest Congress in budgetary savings.

A second obstacle is procedural. The cuts in the spending budget for fiscal 1982 could, in all likelihood, never have been achieved on a bill-by-bill basis. The procedure for the congressional budget resolution made it possible for majorities in the House and Senate to insist on stringent reconciliation instructions for authorizing committees. The reconciliation route then made it possible for committee-by-committee and program-by-program reductions to be packaged together in a comprehensive bill with an up-or-down vote.

The pain still lingers from that vote, and subsequent reconciliation efforts have been considerably less heroic. With the credit budget, however, the procedural supports of budget resolutions, reconciliation, and the like are still in their developmental stage. Whether they will continue to develop—and, equally important, how they will develop—is not at all certain.

Congressional Credit Budgets

The Reagan administration has focused almost exclusively on policy changes as the route to credit control. The dominant effort in Congress has been to develop procedures that would integrate credit into the congressional budget process. In its fiscal 1981 budget resolutions, Congress included nonbinding targets for direct loan and loan guarantee totals. The following year, the non-binding totals were allocated among budget functions. The first fiscal 1983 budget resolution added allocations for committees having jurisdiction over credit programs and, in a major departure, contained enforcement provisions for the credit budget totals included in the resolution. These enforcement provisions were in effect, however, only for the fiscal year covered by the resolution.

The first fiscal 1984 budget resolution returned to nonbinding targets, although it included several sense-of-the-Congress provisions aimed at keeping fiscal 1984 spending within specified levels. As the budget committees have worked on credit budget formats for their annual budget resolutions, they have also considered permanent changes in the budget process that would alter the budgetary treatment of credit programs. While both committees have expressed their support for formal incorporation of credit budgets into areas covered by the 1974 budget act, they have been unwilling thus far to open the act up to amendments. Spending issues have remained so contentious and intercommittee tensions so pronounced that attempts to centralize additional authority within the budget committees would undoubtedly generate strong opposition in Congress.

There has been, then, some improvement in procedures to handle the credit budget over the past several years. It also appears that congressional barriers of indifference to credit control issues are breaking down. Just how meaningful these changes are—and whether progress will continue—is problematical.

The Fiscal 1983 Resolution

The first budget resolution for fiscal 1983 was adopted on 23 June 1982, more than five weeks after the 15 May deadline. That any resolution at all was adopted represented an accomplishment of sorts. On 27 and 28 May, for example, the House rejected eight budget resolution alternatives, including the one reported by its budget committee. On 10 June the House finally adopted a budget resolution, although it once again rejected its budget committee's proposal. Senate action was less chaotic, although here also the budget committee suffered sharp reverses on the floor. A conference agreement was subsequently hammered out by House and Senate Republicans and narrowly approved in both chambers. In the House a coalition of Republicans (156–32) and southern Democrats (40–35) barely prevailed against almost unanimous (14–141) northern Democratic opposition. In the Senate, which adopted the resolution on a 54–45 vote, only three Democrats joined Republicans in support of the conference report.

The debate and coalitions that formed around the first fiscal 1983 resolution suggested a highly conservative fiscal plan. In fact, despite highly questionable economic assumptions and estimates, the fiscal 1983 resolution contained a $100 + billion deficit and an aggregate spending target more than 10 percent above the original fiscal 1982 level. Most of the Reagan administration's proposed domestic spending cuts were rejected, but liberal Democrats were unwilling to accept the defense figures in the fiscal 1983 budget resolution or to agree to the reduced rates of growth for a number of domestic programs. Republicans and conservative Democrats could not generate much enthusiasm for the administration's budget either, although for different reasons. Nevertheless, arguments that a congressional budget—however imperfect—was needed to avoid even more unpleasant fiscal results finally prevailed.

These issues dominated the congressional debate of the fiscal 1983 budget at every stage. The credit budget provisions that were included received very little attention, and much of that was negative. These provisions were first pushed in the House Budget Committee by Democrat Norman Mineta and Republican Ed Bethune. Representative Bethune then convinced other House Republican conferees to insist that credit enforcement provisions be included in the conference agreement.

With respect to its credit provisions, the first concurrent budget resolution went considerably beyond previous congressional actions. First, section 3 of the resolution directed that all new credit authorizations, direct or guaranteed, "shall be effective only to such extent or in such amounts as are contained in appropriation Acts." [25] Second, sections 9(b) and 9(c) required allocations of all new direct loan obligations and loan guarantee commitments (primary and secondary) as set forth in the resolution among the committees of jurisdiction in the House and Senate and directed, for these committees, further allocations among subcommittees. Third, section 9(a) provided for enforcement of the credit budget totals through point-of-order challenges to any credit authorizations that would breach the credit ceiling. This was to make possible the blocking of floor consideration of legislation that would violate the credit budget ceiling. The resolution also stated that, in the event Congress did not complete action on a second concurrent resolution by 1 October 1982, "this concurrent resolution shall be deemed to be the concurrent resolution required to be reported." [26] Since passage of a second resolution by the beginning of fiscal 1982 was considered unlikely, the first resolution's spending and credit targets were intended as ceilings. Because of a drafting error in the budget resolution, the credit targets did not become ceilings on 1 October, but the procedural precedent was established for bringing credit under concurrent budget resolution limits.

The credit budget provisions in the fiscal 1983 resolution followed the allocation and enforcement requirements for direct spending. And in one respect the credit provisions were more stringent. New credit authorizations of any type were subject to appropriations limits. Under section 401 of the 1974 budget act, this same requirement applied to new contract or borrowing authority. With new entitlements that exceeded a committee's allocation, review by the appropriations committees was required, but the committees were empowered only to report an amendment "which limits the total amount of new spending authority provided in such bill or resolution." [27]

In effect, the fiscal 1983 concurrent budget resolution assigned the credit budget the same procedural status as the spending budget, but it did so only for the life of the resolution. Even this temporary advance, however, came under sharp criticism. The chairman of the Senate Appropriations Committee, Mark Hatfield (R-Oregon), argued during debate on the resolution that credit budget enforcement should not be attempted without formally amending the 1974 budget act: "I fully agree that this significant area of Federal economic intervention . . . must be closely examined and brought under some form of better control. I, however, have grave reservations that such a major step should be taken in this resolution. . . . This provision was not included in the

Senate-passed version of the Senate budget resolution and received only cursory attention in the House debate on this amendment." [28] Hatfield's dissatisfaction was shared by the House Appropriations Committee, which complained that it "was not consulted about the mechanics or timing of the new procedure until after the budget resolution was adopted." [29] The committee's report went on to suggest that "perhaps the credit allocations to House committees . . . are in error and will be adjusted." [30]

Despite these complaints, there was actually a good deal of flexibility in the resolution's credit control provisions. The Commodity Credit Corporation, for example, was exempted entirely from the enforcement procedure for credit ceilings. Its lending, along with that of the Veterans Administration, was also exempted from the requirement for appropriations limits on all new credit authorizations, as indeed were all lending authorizations reported prior to adoption of the resolution. In the managers' explanation of the conference report, language was included to discourage the administration from attempting to reduce REA loan programs. [31]

Most important, the lending levels established in the resolution were deliberately set high enough to accommodate all anticipated lending activity during fiscal 1983. Pete Domenici, chairman of the Senate Budget Committee, explained to Senator Hatfield and other critics that Senate conferees had been forced to concede on credit enforcement because it "had been pushed adamantly by a large group of House members whose support for the resolution was crucial." [32] But, Domenici went on to declare, the concession was largely symbolic.

> I agree . . . that a procedural step of this importance should be addressed when we amend the Budget Act, and that it should not be done in an ad hoc kind of way. On the other hand . . . the point of order will create no insurmountable problems this year, because of the numbers in the resolution . . . The amounts in the credit portion are more than ample to cover anticipated credit legislation. . . . We should view this provision largely as a dry-run exercise. This is not a precedent. . . .
> I do not consider this to be in any respect a binding precedent. [33]

The fiscal 1983 congressional credit budget totals were, in fact, sufficiently generous to accommodate current policy lending requirements. [34] They were also well above President Reagan's requests, both for total direct and guaranteed lending and for most budget functions (see Table 6.6). Moreover, no binding precedent was set, for in its fiscal 1984 deliberations, Congress avoided credit enforcement provisions.

Table 6.6 Reagan Administration and Congressional Credit Budgets, by Function, Fiscal Year 1983 (in billions of dollars)

	Direct Loan Obligations		Loan Guarantee Commitments	
Function	President's Budget	Budget Resolution	President's Budget	Budget Resolution
National Defense	-0-	0.05	-0-	0.05
International Affairs	12.2	10.2	7.8	9.3
General Science, Space, and Technology	0.2	0.2	-0-	-0-
Energy	11.2	12.0	-1.8	0.5
Natural Resources and Environment	0.4	0.03	-0-	-0-
Agriculture	13.8	18.1	2.7	2.6
Commerce and Housing Credit	5.9	12.1	37.7	41.0
Transportation	0.1	0.5	0.5	0.8
Community and Regional Development	1.7	2.2	-0.1	0.6
Education, Training, Employment and Social Services	0.6	0.8	10.3	7.2
Health	0.04	0.1	0.1	0.1
Income Security	2.0	2.0	18.7	18.7
Veterans Benefits and Services	0.9	1.0	22.4	20.9
General Government	-0-	0.05	0.01	-0-
General Purpose Fiscal Assistance	0.1	0.2	-0-	0.2
Total[a]	49.0	59.7	98.3	101.9

Source: *Special Analysis F, Federal Credit Programs, Budget of the United States Government, Fiscal Year 1983* (Washington, D.C.: Government Printing Office, 1982), p. 39; Senate Committee on the Budget, *Report No. 97-478, First Concurrent Resolution on the Budget—Fiscal Year 1983* (Washington, D.C.: Government Printing Office, 18 June 1982), p. 31.
a. Totals may not add due to rounding.

The Fiscal 1984 Resolution

The congressional debate on the first concurrent budget resolution for fiscal 1984 was, if anything, more heated and protracted than the previous year's exercise. The Democratic gains in the House in the 1982 elections intensified the conflict over priorities between defense and domestic spending, and the $200 billion deficit projected for fiscal 1984 compounded the difficulty of putting together a budget that could pass the House and Senate. Various sweeteners were used. An "antirecession" reserve fund of up to $18 billion for fiscal years 1984–86 was approved, contingent upon passage of specific program authorizations. Reconciliation instructions were included that barely affected spending but called for $73 billion in additional revenues for the fiscal 1984–86 period. The prospects for these initiatives were not very promising when the first budget resolution was finally adopted in late June, and they did not improve over the next several months. As in fiscal 1983, the fiscal 1984 resolution included language that allowed the first resolution to become binding at the beginning of the fiscal year if no second resoluton had been adopted. This time, however, point-of-order enforcement was limited to budget authority.[35]

What Congress did agree to in the first fiscal 1984 resolution was a series of sense-of-the-Congress provisions that called on the president and Congress to limit, through the appropriations process, new direct and guaranteed lending at levels set in the resolution and to hold purchases of guaranteed loans and certificates of beneficial ownership by the Federal Financing Bank to specified levels as well. A third provision, also nonbinding, called for borrowing transactions of federal agencies to be restricted as much as possible to the FFB.

The budgetary problems associated with the FFB received special attention in the fiscal 1984 resolution. Section 9 suggested that "the budgets of Federal agencies initiating Federal Financing Bank purchases of certificates of beneficial ownership and originations of guaranteed loans should include the budget authority and outlays resulting from the transactions."[36] It went on to recommend that committees having jursidiction over the Federal Financing Bank Act of 1973 "consider expeditiously" legislation to require these budget-accounting changes beginning with the fiscal 1985 budget.

All of these sense-of-the-Congress provisions originated in the Senate, as did a provision not accepted in conference requiring committee and subcommittee allocations of the credit budget totals. House Budget Committee Republicans, who had pushed for credit enforcement provisions the previous year, had virtually no impact on the House-passed version of the fiscal 1984 resolution, and no House Republicans signed the subsequent conference report. There was, indeed, very little Republican support in either chamber for the budget plan that emerged from conference. With President Reagan denouncing the spending and tax numbers in the conference agreement, only 10 House Republicans and 19 Senate Republicans voted to adopt the first concurrent resolution for fiscal 1984. Overwhelming Democratic support, however, was sufficient to pass the resolution.

The first round of the fiscal 1984 budget debate did not assign great prominence to credit. With survival of the congressional budget process at issue, as it was in the spring of 1983, the retreat on credit enforcement was not difficult to understand. Moreover, the sense-of-the-Congress provisions provided at least a modest endorsement of FFB reforms. It was clear, however, that no consensus had formed on congressional credit policy.

Credit Expansion

Congressional credit budgets have not, at least thus far, forced substantial policy reductions. Where used, appropriations limits for individual programs have been set sufficiently high to cover all anticipated lending. According to the Congressional Budget Office:

> The credit budget procedures . . . have emphasized appropriations limits as the effective control for the credit budget. A review of the actual direct loan obligations and loan guarantee commitments for 1981 and 1982 shows that for a substantial number of programs there were large gaps between program . . . limits and the obligations and commitments. To some extent these program shortfalls were due to the recession. In other cases the limits have been set too high to exert any real control over program levels.[37]

In addition, the credit budget aggregates have probably helped to shield individual programs from administration attacks. For lending programs already on the books, then, the congressional credit budgets have had minimal impact. What the credit budget mechanism has done, however, is make it more difficult to enact major new credit programs.

This was illustrated by the remarkable House turnaround on the proposed Defense Base Revitalization Act of 1982, which would have provided massive amounts of new credit to small and medium-sized businesses. The Economic Stabilization Subcommittee of the House Banking Committee reported the bill by a vote of 19–3 on 24 March 1982. It was then approved by a large, bipartisan majority of the full House Banking Committee and approved as well by the Education and Labor Committee. The latter had jurisdiction over the measure's job-training grants totaling $1.75 billion over five years, but the heart of the legislation was up to $5 billion for the net costs of loan guarantees, direct loans, purchase contracts, and price guarantees for fiscal years 1983–87. Cost estimates by the Congressional Budget Office projected $2.3 billion in new loan guarantee commitments each year and a default rate over 20 percent.[38] During House floor debate, estimates of up to $50 billion in loan guarantees were not challenged by the bill's supporters.[39]

The vehicle for this program was a reauthorization of the 1950 Defense Production Act, the same measure that the Nixon administration unsuccessfully proffered to assist the Lockheed Corporation. House Democrats, who had blocked the Nixon effort, this time found the Defense Production Act an appropriate umbrella, despite evidence that much of the support provided would be for nonmilitary purposes.[40] In any case, it appeared that the measure would easily pass the House as an antirecession initiative.

On the floor, however, the legislation was caught in budget process arguments. The direct spending authorizations ran up against the functional allocations for national defense and were attacked by Armed Services Committee members, who had not reported or reviewed the legislation. Moreover, Representative Bethune, who had led the fight to include credit budget enforcement in the fiscal 1983 budget resolution pointed out that the credit allocation for the defense function could not accommodate the amount of new credit authority contemplated in the bill. "We put in [the credit budget] a very small amount for the defense function," Bethune stated, "because we decided, looking at the macroeconomic picture, that we did not want to allocate any more for the defense function at this particular time." [41]

Proponents were more than willing to concede that very large sums of new credit were at stake. Democratic Majority Leader Jim Wright agreed that the bill "spends about $5 billion and in so doing it leverages the private expenditure of another $50 billion. I think that is the best argument you could make for the bill." [42] Moreover, Wright argued, credit assistance was really cost-free. New federal lending simply continued "the historic pattern that has been so successful in this country. . . . Loan guarantees and guaranteed purchases [have] not cost us in the past." [43]

After two days of debate, the House finally approved an amendment that effectively killed the measure. In response to questions about the economic impact of credit assistance, the House accepted language that prohibited new lending if the Treasury Department determined it would lead to higher interest rates or harm the thrift industry. The Republican-sponsored amendment gained the support of almost all House Republicans (135–16) and enough Democrats to pass by a 173–154 margin.

House Democrats resurrected their "defense-stimulus" bill again in 1983, although at greatly reduced levels. With economic recovery underway, Republican opposition should again prevail in the House and will almost certainly block Senate action. Congressional Democrats, however, are considering much more ambitious undertakings as a prelude to the 1984 elections.

The most prominent of these is a proposal for a national industrial development bank, modeled on the Reconstruction Finance Corporation. As proposed by House Democrats David E. Bonior (D-Mich.) and Stan Lundine (D-N.Y.), the bank would initially be able to provide up to $12 billion in direct loans and

$24 billion in loan guarantees to support low-cost credit to key industries. Other proposals before the House Banking Committee's Economic Stabilization Subcommittee are also tied to Democratic support for a national industrial policy, in which credit assistance would play a major role. Advocates of these proposals received a small boost when the first fiscal 1984 budget resolution included a $50 million reserve for the as yet unauthorized development bank.

The Ninety-eighth Congress has also debated a number of more limited credit assistance proposals. Among these are private mortgage aid, a merchant marine development bank, additional Amtrak support, and a lending authority to assist the Washington Public Power Supply System (WPPSS), which defaulted on $2.25 billion of construction bonds on 25 July 1983. While the congressional credit budget has not in any sense blocked congressional action on these or similar proposals, it has at least made it more difficult to ignore real or potential costs. When the rescue attempt for WPPSS reached the Senate floor, for example, critics pointed to the enormous subsidies already provided to the Northwest power system. Over $7 billion has been loaned to the Bonneville Power Administration, which backed the WPPSS bonds, by the Treasury at interest rates of 1 to 2 percent. Even with this assistance, the loans have been frequently rescheduled, and only $43 million of the $7 billion debt repaid. Federal Energy Regulatory Commission estimates put the current repayment delay costs to the Treasury at $740 million to $1.4 billion.[44]

The variety of new credit proposals, and the widespread Democratic support for a federal industrial policy, is ample evidence that credit assistance remains an attractive policy option. Over the short term, the Reagan administration's opposition to federal credit allocations has precluded any substantial expansion of federal credit activity. Without that opposition, the congressional credit budget procedures in place over the past several years might have been tested more severely, but the procedures have clearly provided some independent restraint. At the same time, decisions that would make credit budget enforcement permanent have been avoided, so that future restraint is far from certain.

Credit Policy and Procedures

Compared to the spending budget, the credit budget appears to be under "control." Federal lending has remained within budgeted levels the past three years, and this is likely to continue through at least fiscal 1984. How much of this control is deliberate—and permanent—is another matter. In its enforcement procedures the credit budget is weaker than the spending budget, and all of the major credit programs have survived the Reagan credit budgets reasonably intact. The momentum of credit programs already in place remains formidable and, unless slowed drastically, will continue to support a significant federal role in credit allocation.

The Reagan administration's policy emphasis and the budget committees' procedural focus have helped to direct greater attention to federal credit activities. Budgetary treatment of federal credit, however, remains confusing and unsatisfactory. If credit control is to be more than an occasional accident, the policy and procedural issues relating to budgetary treatment must finally be resolved. They must be resolved, moreover, so that the real costs of federal credit are finally reflected in the budget.

Chapter 7
Controlling Federal Credit

Federal credit intervention goes back at least to the 1930s, but its scope and impact remained fairly limited until the 1970s. During that decade, credit programs proliferated wildly, with federal credit activity variously justified "as a technique for relieving poverty, equalizing opportunity, promoting economic growth, fighting inflation, creating jobs, or even improving the balance of payments."[1] All of this could be accomplished, moreover, at little or no direct budgetary cost, which encouraged the illusion that credit assistance was somehow cost-free.

Over the past several years, the situation has changed. Federal credit activity now receives much greater attention in the executive branch and Congress; credit budgets have been initiated; and as legislators have gained some idea of the economic effects and hidden costs of credit programs, they have allotted them at least modest status on the policy agenda.

Despite these positive changes, the budgetary treatment of credit programs remains seriously deficient. For a variety of reasons, the budgetary treatment of credit programs is demonstrably less rigorous than that of direct spending. The first set of problems associated with federal credit, then, relates to the accuracy and comprehensiveness of the unified budget. The distortions introduced by credit programs make it much more difficult to assess the total resources used by government or their allocation among competing purposes and programs.[2] Under current practices, credit programs represent a fiscal subterfuge of major proportions, making it much harder for government to practice—and voters to judge—fiscal responsibility.

Off-budget agencies, loan guarantees, and government-sponsored enterprises are, in political terms, quite similar. They allow the federal government to evade political constraints on its taxing and spending activities.[3] They allow servicing of the organized in obscure and complex ways. The occasional public controversies—such as those surrounding the Lockheed, Chrysler, and New York City loan programs—are the exceptions. The tens of billions in routine credit activity each year are the rule.

A second set of problems is economic. Federal credit programs affect the allocation and cost of credit, but there is a good deal of uncertainty about the magnitude and direction of these effects. Unfortunately, and despite a good deal of speculation, there is no clear-cut evidence about the impact of federal credit intervention on capital markets in general.[4] There is even disagreement about how individual programs affect submarkets, such as housing.[5]

Federal credit control therefore poses an unusual challenge. Like spending assistance or tax preferences, credit programs provide benefits that are tangible, immediate, and concentrated. But while spending and tax policy are subject to at least some scrutiny regarding totals, allocations, and especially deficits, credit budget totals lack equivalent political and economic symbolism.

The central issue, then, is how to correct these imbalances and thereby facilitate credit control. There are several available options, ranging from the simple abolition of off-budget agencies to a major restructuring of the federal budget. In analyzing the various proposals, however, it is helpful to keep in mind Aaron Wildavsky's dictum that "there would be no point in tinkering with the budget machinery if, at the end, the pattern of budgetary decisions was precisely the same as before. On the contrary, reform has little justification unless it results in different kinds of decisions."[6] Credit "controls" that do not constrain credit behavior will do little to improve our understanding of how programs operate, what they actually cost, or what role the government can effectively perform in credit markets.

Formalizing the Credit Budget

During both the Ninety-seventh and Ninety-eighth Congresses, legislation has been introduced to establish a permanent, statutory basis for controlling direct loans and loan guarantees. Through formal amendments to the 1974 budget act, federal credit activities would be incorporated into the congressional budget process. This would make the budget process more comprehensive, with parallel treatment of spending and credit totals in congressional budget resolutions and appropriate enforcement measures to make the totals "binding."

The leading House proponents of a formal credit budget have been representatives Norman Mineta and Ed Bethune. Senator Charles Percy, who participated in the development of the 1974 budget act, has led the drive for a credit budget in the Senate. Despite strong cosponsorship in both chambers, credit budget legislation has moved very slowly. Part of the delay can be attributed to multiple committee referrals: four separate standing committees are involved on the House side alone. In addition, since credit control advocates have been able to achieve some of their objectives through ad hoc changes in the budget process, a good deal of the pressure for formal modification has been dissipated. Most important, however, the future of the budget process itself is a matter of widespread uncertainty.

The House Rules Committee, for example, has made incorporation of the credit budget part of its two-year task force examination of the entire budget process, but there has been little progress in fashioning a consensus in the House as to how, and indeed if, the overall process should be strengthened. In the Senate, the leadership of the budget committee has been reluctant to propose formal amendments in what it views as an increasingly unpopular and vulnerable budget process.[7] This reluctance was probably reinforced when a Senate-commissioned study report issued in the spring of 1983 by former senators James B. Pearson and Abraham Ribicoff recommended abolishing the budget committees and scrapping part of the budget process.

The Spending Control Model

While there is a good deal of disagreement about the merits of the 1974 budget act, its provisions for spending control provide the goal-setting and enforcement mechanisms that most congressional proponents of credit control favor. The first concurrent budget resolution for each fiscal year establishes target spending aggregates—for outlays and budget authority—and allocates these aggregates among the functional categories of the budget and the spending committees. These aggregates become binding ceilings upon adoption of a second resolution or, as provided in the first budget resolutions for fiscal 1983 and 1984, upon a specified date if no second resolution is adopted. Once the spending ceiling is in effect, spending bills that would violate the ceiling can be blocked from floor consideration through point-of-order challenges.

As the budget process has evolved, the budget committees have attempted to strengthen interim conformity to spending goals rather than wait for violations of second resolution ceilings. One of the routine procedures upon which they depend is scorekeeping, in which the legislative actions of the spending committees, especially the appropriations committees, are tracked in relation to the functional and committee allocations contained in the first budget resolution. While there are no automatic sanctions against committees or spending bills that violate the resolution, the budget committees have used occasional floor challenges to encourage compliance.[8] In addition, the first fiscal 1984 resolution contained a new procedure for enforcing spending ceilings on the basis of spending committee allocations. The extensive use of continuing resolutions over the past several years has complicated the scorekeeping procedure, but the budget committees have been able to protect discretionary spending goals reasonably well.[9]

A second and decidedly more controversial enforcement mechanism is reconciliation. This involves budget resolution instructions to House and Senate committees to report legislation producing a specified amount of spending reductions (or theoretically increases) for a given fiscal year or multiyear period. Committees have discretion over which programs to cut, but are required to achieve designated legislative savings. They must also report out the necessary changes by the deadline specified in the budget resolution. Various committee actions may then be combined in a single reconciliation bill, managed by the budget committees. Although reconciliation was originally viewed as an enforcement adjunct of the second budget resolution, it has been used since 1981 in conjunction with the first resolution, primarily to effect changes in entitlement spending and tax policy.[10]

What the congressional budget process allows—but does not guarantee—is conformity between the aggregate and allocation goals set forth in congressional budget resolutions and congressional action on spending (and tax) measures. It has worked reasonably well for discretionary spending controlled on an annual basis through the appropriations process. It has worked considerably less well for entitlements and other nondiscretionary spending. As a result, during fiscal years 1980–83, aggregate spending far exceeded the levels set in first concurrent budget resolutions. For outlays, the average annual error was approximately $40 billion, while actual budget authority enacted each year was more than $25 billion greater, on average, than budget resolution levels. As a result, average annual outlay growth for this four-year period averaged almost 13 percent, while budget authority lagged only slightly behind, at just over 11 percent annually.

It is entirely possible, of course, that spending would have grown even more rapidly in the absence of these spending control procedures and the elaborate congressional budget process. But the recent pattern is unmistakable—low rates of spending growth in first resolutions, when public attention is at its peak, followed by greatly revised resolutions a year later to accommodate much higher growth. The revised resolution is then overshadowed by the highly publicized, "tight" first resolution for the upcoming fiscal year.

Congress's experience with spending control suggests that spending totals are important but not determinative. They have symbolic value, especially in association with deficits, but it is not at all clear that violations of spending totals have negative political consequences. Since a similar uncertainty exists about fiscal consequences, it is not difficult to understand the remarkable flexibility exhibited by spending budgets. With credit budgets, the totals are, if anything, even more arbitrary, which does not inspire great confidence about disciplined credit behavior.

The Credit Control Analog

Incorporating the credit budget into the congressional budget process would entail goal-setting and enforcement procedures that generally parallel those for spending. Under current proposals, standing committees would be required to report estimates of lending under their jurisdiction to the budget committees by 15 March. In a departure from the spending model, the budget committees would receive as well a recommended credit total from the House and Senate banking committees.

The first concurrent budget resolution reported by the House and Senate budget committees would then include (in addition to the "appropriate budgetary levels" for revenues, spending, deficit, and debt currently provided) "appropriate levels of total Federal credit activity" for upcoming fiscal years, with the total subdivided for direct loan obligations and loan guarantee commitments.[11] These subtotals would in turn be allocated among the functional categories in the budget. The conference report on the first resolution would also set forth the corresponding allocations among House and Senate committees. The post–first resolution steps would follow the spending enforcement format. Scorekeeping would be applied to credit legislation, although this would probably require that the definition of budget authority be expanded to include loan guarantees. Reconciliation could be used to instruct committees to alter credit legislation. Measures that would violate the credit ceiling would be subject to point-of-order challenges. Finally, credit estimates would be required in new legislation, and newly enacted credit authority would be contingent upon appropriation acts. This last provision has previously been applied to contract and borrowing authority under the 1974 budget act.

One important difference between spending and credit is that the latter uses a hierarchy to prevent double counting when credit programs are aggregated. Direct loans are "ranked above" loan guarantees, so that FFB purchases of agency loan guarantees are counted as direct loans in the credit budget. Credit budget enforcement would therefore have to be applied separately to direct lending and loan guarantees.

With these procedures in place, credit budgets could be adopted and enforced. Incorporation of a separate credit budget into the 1974 budget act framework would provide binding credit totals, scorekeeping enforcement, reconciliation instructions for credit programs, and, if necessary, point-of-order enforcement against credit measures that violate credit ceilings. In addition, some of the off-budget accounting problems that now exist would be remedied. All off-budget credit activity would be included in the credit budget, regardless of the budgetary status of lending agencies. The FFB's lending activities would be indirectly controlled by the gross limits and accompanying allocations for direct loan obligations and loan guarantee commitments.

Supplementary Budgetary Changes

A comprehensive congressional budget process—with separate spending, tax, and credit aggregates—would represent an improvement in federal budgeting. It would almost certainly increase the visibility of credit programs. It might eventually encourage greater scrutiny of program management. There are, however, several problems of varying difficulty associated with this approach. While off-budget agencies would be included in the credit budget, their outlays would not be reflected in spending or deficit totals. In the case of the FFB, outlays arising from the bank's operations would not be attributed to originating agencies. Repealing the legal provisions—such as section 11(c) of the Federal Financing Bank Act of 1973—that exclude off-budget entities from unified budget totals would remove current distortions and inconsistencies in budgetary treatment. Attribution of FFB outlays to originating agencies would clarify the allocation of budgetary resources.

It would also be possible to solve the distinctive problems associated with the FFB in another fashion, that is, by revising the budgetary treatment of CBOs and direct loans to guaranteed borrowers. Changing current law to redefine CBO sales as borrowing, as recommended by the Reagan administration, would eliminate the transferring of on-budget loans to off-budget status. Agencies would still show the outlay costs of new direct loans, regardless of CBO sales to the FFB. A similar approach could be applied to FFB purchases of loan guarantees by on-budget agencies. By treating these as direct loans by the agency issuing the guarantee and the FFB transaction as agency borrowing, agency budgets would accurately reflect the budget authority and outlays associated with FFB-financed direct loans.

Repealing off-budget exemptions and either directly or indirectly dealing with the FFB markedly improves the accuracy of unified budget spending and deficit totals as well as spending priorities. These steps would equalize the competition for resources by ending the favored status of off-budget credit (and spending) agencies. And, in conjunction with the credit budget, congressional control over credit allocation would be greatly strengthened.

Incorporating the credit budget also raises the question of the impoundment of loan guarantees. Congress's past willingness to adopt mandatory language for loan guarantee programs suggests that impoundment controls will be a necessary part of any formal credit budget procedure. At the same time, the Supreme Court's rejection of the legislative veto in *Immigration and Natural-*

ization Service v. *Chadha*, decided on 23 June 1983, raises questions about the deferral procedure in Title 10 of the 1974 Impoundment Control Act. It is likely that some change will be necessary in the one-house veto provisions for proposed spending deferrals submitted by the president. The rescission procedure, which requires enactment of new legislation to cancel existing budget authority, does not appear to be affected by the court's decision. The probability, then, is that existing rescission controls will be applied to loan guarantees, and a modified deferral control will be developed for both spending and loan guarantees.

None of these seemingly technical issues is trivial. Each has policy implications. Each affects executive or congressional control of budget decisions. It is also possible that the elimination of off-budget status for agencies or agency attribution of FFB lending might be enacted independently of a budget act revision. Indeed, even if a full-scale budget revision were not forthcoming, these types of reforms would represent a significant improvement in the budget process. For those budgetary changes that would supplement budget incorporation, concrete legislative solutions exist.

Protecting the Totals

A much more complicated problem is how to set—and then to protect—credit budget totals. The primary concern with credit budget totals is, after all, their economic impact, both for capital markets in general and particular credit submarkets. In preparing their recommendations to the budget committees, for example, the House and Senate banking committees would presumably be looking for an "appropriate" level of federal credit intervention. In reconciling these totals with the credit demands of other committees, the budget committees would need to arrive at a recommended level for all new credit activity. It is not at all clear, however, how this level should be measured, much less set.

The federal participation rate—which measures funds advanced under federal auspices against total funds advanced in domestic credit markets—is a convenient yardstick and has the advantage of long-term use. Whether it provides much assistance in setting credit budget totals, however, is debatable. As reported in the past, the participation rate includes the lending activities of government-sponsored enterprises. While it would be easy for Congress to utilize a participation rate that excludes the enterprises, that rate would be hard to defend as inherently meaningful, especially since lending by government-sponsored enterprises could fluctuate without any congressional control.

The participation rate may be the best measure available, but it is subject to so many caveats that Congress would be hard-pressed to use it to force credit program reductions. And this is the key difficulty. Unless the economic impact of a given credit total or participation rate is perceived as substantial and reasonably predictable, the incentives to defend aggregate levels against programmatic demands diminish rather rapidly.

Similar, but actually less complicated, problems have affected the spending budget. One of the reasons that Congress reformed its budget process in 1974 was to enable it to determine fiscal policy through spending and revenue totals. The budget that Congress uses for fiscal policy "management"—the unified budget—is not an especially suitable instrument for that purpose. Since it does not include off-budget spending, it is not particularly unified. More to the point, the most suitable instrument for assessing the economic impact of federal budget policy is the national income accounts. This is reported in the special analyses supplement to the annual budget. As noted in the 1984 edition, "No single budget concept can satisfy all . . . purposes fully. . . . For a study of aggregate economic activity, however, the national income and product accounts (NIA) . . . provide the most useful measure." [12]

But of course Congress does not set a spending total based on some fiscal design and then proceed to decide functional and programmatic allocations. The budget committees have traditionally decided spending levels for each budget function and then adopted corresponding outlay and budget authority aggregates. [13] There are, upon occasion, reductions if the aggregates appear "too high," but the aggregates are not the product of deliberate fiscal policy planning. The subsequent disparities between budget resolution aggregates and actual spending levels, moreover, are typically attributed to unanticipated economic factors. What this really means, regardless of the rhetoric about fiscal policy management, is that the economy drives the budget, and economic conditions are notoriously hard to predict. [14] The economic significance of a given spending total, or for that matter a given deficit total, is uncertain. The political consequences are likewise problematical. With neither the substantive economic nor political implications of spending totals clear-cut, Congress's willingness to sacrifice the totals in order to preserve popular spending programs is easy to understand. In a rare example of congressional humility, Senator William Proxmire made the point that "no matter how thorough or careful our economic analysis may be, the best we can do is guess whether a particular Federal policy tossed into the huge vastness of this $3 trillion economy will end up pushing employment up, or interest rates down." [15]

Why then should Congress be more willing to defend credit budget totals against pressures to lend than it has been to defend spending totals against pressures to spend? There is no compelling evidence about market effects.

There is nothing in the credit budget comparable to deficits in the public's concern. And there is the additional difficulty that the economic effects of different types of lending are more variable than is the case for spending.

While the macroeconomic effects of various types of spending may differ, depending upon what the money is spent for or who receives it, the differences are sufficiently modest that they are usually ignored.[16] Therefore, the *composition* of the spending budget has a political and programmatic relevance that greatly outweighs its economic impact.

For credit programs, variable economic effects are difficult to ignore. As Elisabeth H. Rhyne explains, the composition of the credit budget is of major importance:

> Some supporters of the credit budget as a control device hope that the macroeconomics of federal credit will soon become well enough understood that the "right" aggregate level can be chosen. . . . However, because subsidies differ, the fiscal implications of a credit budget made up largely of near-market FHA-insured mortgages would differ sharply from one containing the same volume of mortgages made under the Farmers Home Administration's low-interest Rural Housing Insurance Fund. The credit budget framework is useful, but it cannot yet offer much assistance in setting macroeconomic policy.[17]

A formal credit budget, together with more accurate budgetary treatment of credit programs, will improve the congressional and executive decision-making processes, but it will not provide a clear-cut basis for control. It may be possible, however, to provide that control by focusing on credit subsidies.

"Costing" Federal Credit

The credit budget attempts to control the gross volume of new lending. If appropriate modifications in the treatment of off-budget agencies are made, the unified budget can "control" the outlays resulting from net direct lending (and loan guarantee defaults). A free-standing credit budget and the unified budget, while not entirely independent of each other, provide alternative ways to measure credit activities. They do not, however, adequately measure the subsidy costs of credit programs, and this measurement may represent the best single means of controlling credit activity.

Two facets of credit program costs can serve as control points. The first is the interest subsidy provided by a direct loan or a loan guarantee. The second involves the default and delinquency costs in the administration of credit programs. By integrating these costs into the unified budget, it becomes possible to force trade-offs between spending and credit assistance, to shatter the illusion that the latter are cost-free, and to provide decision makers with incentives to scrutinize and control credit activity.

Integrating Credit and Spending

It is generally agreed that credit and direct spending are not sufficiently comparable—in programmatic or economic terms—to allow simple dollar-for-dollar budgeting trade-offs. The *costs* of credit are not necessarily the same as the *amount* of credit. The costs of direct spending, for all intents and purposes, are the same as the budget amount. In order to integrate budgetary decisions on spending and credit in a meaningful fashion, it is necessary to provide a direct spending equivalent for a given credit program level. This can be done by estimating the present volume of the interest subsidy: "the equivalent cash grant value of a federal loan or loan guarantee." [18]

This interest subsidy is not just the difference between the interest rate charged by the government and the government's own borrowing costs. Rather, it is determined by the difference between the loan terms a borrower receives under a federal credit program and the loan terms that same borrower would face in private credit markets without federal assistance. If there were private market surrogates for every federal credit program, interest subsidies could be readily and reliably measured on a program-by-program basis. Many federal programs have no private market equivalents, however, and in some instances federally assisted borrowers are such high risks that private credit might not be available under any circumstances. The estimating problem associated with the latter would be especially pronounced for single-borrower and high-risk guarantee programs.

There are difficulties with this measurement of interest subsidy, but they are not insuperable. Over the past several years, for example, the Congressional Budget Office has introduced what are now widely accepted techniques for bill costing—estimating the long-term costs of pending legislation—and assessing the impact on inflation of new legislation. [19] It has recently begun to provide interest subsidy estimates as well. [20] The OMB has for years reported interest subsidies for direct loan programs and selected guarantee programs. It would require cooperation between the executive and legislative branches to develop the necessary technical conventions and budgetary definitions for comprehensive subsidy estimates (that is, not just obvious interest subsidies but considerations of risk and loan terms as well) across all credit programs, but the potential improvement in both budgetary processes would appear sufficiently significant to encourage this type of cooperation.

This focus on subsidies is hardly a new idea. The 1955 Hoover Commission recommended that lending agencies be charged for interest subsidies by the Treasury.[21] The 1961 Report of the Committee on Money and Credit also stressed that deliberate subsidies be identified for all credit programs.[22] President Kennedy's Committee on Federal Credit Programs recommended that "all proposals to create new credit programs or to broaden existing credit programs should be accompanied by an appraisal of the relationship between the interest rate charged in the program, the rate which would be charged by competitive and efficient private lenders and the rate necessary to cover the Government's costs. . . . The normal reviews of all existing Federal credit programs should include discussion of these relationships."[23] The 1967 President's Commission on Budget Concepts suggested that separate budget presentations for loans and direct spending be included in the budget in order to facilitate analysis of their respective impact "on incomes and employment."[24] It emphasized, however, that the subsidy costs in credit programs should be included in the spending budget:

> A surplus or deficit should therefore be presented in the budget, to be calculated by comparing expenditures other than loans with total budget receipts, for purposes of providing a measure of the economic impact of Federal programs. However, the subsidy elements in all such loans should be included and specifically disclosed in the expenditure rather than the loan account . . . since such subsidies are much more like grants than loans. This will make a meaningful separation of loans from other budget expenditures possible. Measurement of the subsidy in loans would reflect both the interest rate subsidy, capitalized at the time the loan is made, and the provision of adequate allowances for losses.[25]

The present value of the interest subsidy differs widely among credit programs currently in place. The rural housing program, for example, is heavily subsidized, while veterans housing loans are not. A recent estimate of their spending equivalencies shows each rural housing dollar as, in effect, a grant worth 68 cents, compared to only 3 cents for every veterans housing dollar.[26] For direct loan programs, existing subsidies are heavily concentrated in a relatively few programs, even using the OMB's conservative market rate discount estimates (see Table 7.1). Since large subsidy disparities also characterize loan guarantee programs, a reasonably similar degree of concentration is likely there as well.[27] Integrating credit subsidies into the spending budget, then, will focus executive and congressional attention on the comparatively small number of programs that do substitute large hidden subsidies for direct assistance. This will, in turn, foster greater competition and certainly more equal competition for assistance dollars.

Table 7.1 Interest Subsidy Values, Selected Direct Loan Programs, 1983 (in billions of dollars)

Direct Loan Program	Obligations	Present Value of Subsidy Stream	Subsidy as Percentage of Obligations
Agricultural Credit	$ 4.3	$0.75	17%
Rural Housing	3.4	2.15	63%
Farm Export Credits	0.75	0.4	53%
Rural Electric/Telephone	1.3	0.7	54%
Housing for Elderly or Handicapped	0.6	0.2	33%
Export-Import Bank	3.8	0.7	18%
Federal Financing Bank	27.0	4.3	16%
Total	$41.1	$9.2	22%
Percentage of Total Direct Loan Programs	67%	82%	

Source: *Special Analysis F, Federal Credit Programs, Budget of the United States Government, Fiscal Year 1984* (Washington, D.C.: Congressional Budget Office, 1983), pp. F-57–F-58.

Default Costs

The appraisal of interest subsidies should take into account risk, which means that spending "charges" would be assessed prospectively for defaults and delinquencies. It is difficult to assess risk for many programs because of the lack of private sector equivalencies. It is also difficult because risk and related program costs are obscured by current agency reporting systems.[28] Standardized and comprehensive reporting of defaults needs to be implemented for all credit programs simply as a prerequisite for effective programmatic oversight, quite apart from credit budget reforms.[29]

Despite sporadic efforts by the executive branch to improve reporting on defaults and delinquencies, default criteria and definitions vary substantially from agency to agency.[30] Rescheduling of delinquent loans is a widespread practice. Agencies that apply default criteria strictly are penalized for doing so in their budget figures, while laxity and obfuscation are in effect rewarded. If the executive branch and Congress are serious about credit control, changes in budgeting formats need to be complemented by program information that can support policy decisions. This type of information is now lacking, and here again cooperation between the two branches will be necessary if any substantial improvements are to be achieved.

Once interest subsidies, including default risk, are integrated into the unified budget, a solid basis for credit control could be established. Instead of disembodied credit totals, whose chief contribution to credit control consists of sheer size and *possible* economic effects, credit budget totals would have tangible and immediate budgetary costs. This would not guarantee control, but it would at least provide incentives for control, which now appear to be almost nonexistent.

It is conceivable, moreover, that subsidy estimates would allow totally separate budgets for expenditures and lending, as the 1967 Budget Concept Commission recommended and former Congressional Budget Office director Alice Rivlin recently endorsed. Rivlin has suggested, in fact, that the federal budget be broken down into three components: direct spending, direct loans, and loan guarantees.[31] Each of these would be matched against its appropriate offsets: taxes against direct spending; loan repayments against direct loans; and expiring guarantees against new loan guarantees. This would provide, argues Rivlin, much more comprehensive and accurate information about the extent and forms of federal assistance and about economic impact. It would direct attention "not towards one budget deficit of ambiguous interpretation, but towards two or more clear-cut measures—deficit spending and net credit extensions being the most important."[32]

Whether this type of drastic restructuring is desirable, it makes sense only if the spending subsidies hidden in credit programs are included in the expenditure section. Integrating credit and spending, therefore, does not require a single budget presentation. It may be preferable for analytical purposes to utilize separate credit and spending formats, but only because credit involves a financial component (an exchange of assets) that spending does not. The subsidy component of federal credit, however, is spending, not an exchange of assets. It belongs, accordingly, with other forms of direct spending assistance.

The Politics of Credit

Requiring the inclusion of credit subsidy costs in the unified budget would alter the politics of credit programs. What makes credit assistance unique, after all, is not that the programs are really "hidden" (or unduly complex or inherently inefficient or inevitably flawed) but rather that the *costs* are difficult to measure. As a consequence, there are no established norms that constrain political decision makers or established "guardians" that are responsible for credit control. The evidence is reasonably clear that credit assistance has frequently been used instead of direct spending or tax preferences because its financial costs tend to be sufficiently diffuse, uncertain, and indirect (as well as often being long-term) to shelter political benefits against political costs.

With credit, there need be no losers. Presidents and members of Congress must face the budgetary consequences of additional spending or foregone revenue. So long as the norm of a balanced budget was accepted at the federal level, politically tolerable levels of taxation acted as a natural restraint on spending pressures. While the balanced budget norm has been ignored for quite some time, it at least commands a good deal of public acceptance and cannot be explicitly dismissed by political leaders. There is, however, no corresponding norm that governs credit. Credit levels need not be balanced or even measured against some desirable, meaningful standard. Like deficit financing, credit programs are an irresistible temptation for hard-pressed public officials, since they do not impose immediate, direct costs on taxpayers. In addition, credit programs do not compete directly with other types of spending. The absence of established norms, as Wildavsky emphasizes, is a bias in favor of advocacy and against control:

> No one can compare an appropriation to a direct loan, to a guarantee, or to any of a number of other spending devices. The decline of comprehensiveness weakens control. Ignorant of how much is being spent, central budget offices are less able to say that any amount . . . is too much. Looking good, as opposed to doing well, becomes tempting for guardians as well as advocates. . . . Without rules that equate all major forms of spending, accounting sleight of hand substitutes for spending control. Naturally, program advocates are more than willing to play this game.[33]

The strategies employed by advocates of credit programs, are not unusual. Initially, they justify credit assistance as a temporary response to an emergency situation. Once a program is established, they can shift the emphasis to broadening the beneficiary class and increasing benefit levels. When a base of political support is established, the "burden of proof" transfers to program opponents, who must explain why a popular, ongoing program should be cut. None of this is very different from the typical scenario for spending programs or tax preferences.

If advocacy strategies are fairly uniform for the different types of spending and credit programs, opposition strategies are not. The fiscal yardsticks that can be employed against spending or tax initiatives are straightforward. Voting against new spending or tax cuts, for example, will reduce spending and deficit totals or, alternatively, will make resources available for other purposes. With credit programs, opposition appeals must generally be more abstract. There may be, after all, no outlay or deficit consequences if guaranteed loans or off-budget direct loans are used to channel assistance. Dollars of credit saved do not mean equivalent spending, deficit, or tax savings. They may mean lower interest rates or more efficient uses of capital, but these effects are difficult to demonstrate, especially with any degree of precision.

The political incentives to oppose credit, therefore, are weak. They become even weaker when real crises affect major sectors of the economy or large companies. The costs of not extending credit—reckoned in unemployment, increased social welfare spending, reduced government revenue, and the like—are sufficiently manipulable that even modestly inventive advocates can argue that more credit assistance actually means saving the government money. The unemployment figures tossed out during the more publicized bailouts of the past decade may have been grossly exaggerated, but they were effective. That many of the jobs in question would soon disappear regardless of federal assistance (and, in fact, had to disappear for profitability or solvency to be restored) was rarely mentioned.

All of this complicates the task of guardianship, particularly in Congress, where there are no established "control committees." The budget committees and appropriations committees have begun to develop procedures for centralizing credit decision making, but it is unclear that they will be willing or able to restrain substantially the growth of federal credit assistance. Until now, credit "ceilings" have been deliberately generous, and the objective of credit budgets has been primarily to educate members of Congress. At what point in the education process members of Congress will be ready to support control committees against advocacy committees is uncertain, but the history of spending control efforts in Congress does not inspire a great deal of confidence about the prospects for credit control.

Moreover, the accounting conventions currently used for credit programs do not provide the budget or appropriations committees with a commensurate stake in serious credit control efforts. Since budgetary costs are, for many credit programs, hidden or obscure, program reductions will not provide much in the way of budgetary savings. Once again, the lack of incentives associated with credit control comes into play, and it creates a decided bias against control committees.

The politics of credit programs, then, is characterized by inadequate constraints. Closing the fiscal loophole for credit programs requires, in Wildavsky's formulation, "rules that equate all major forms of spending."[34] And chief among these is the measurement of credit subsidy costs. It is important to recognize that this need not lead to across-the-board credit reductions.

Credit assistance may in some instances be a desirable alternative to direct spending assistance, but this type of decision should be guided by programmatic considerations rather than "accounting sleight of hand." At the same time, it is likely that many credit assistance programs would be reduced or eliminated once subsidy costs were an integral part of the decision-making process. Many agriculture programs, for example, will become considerably more visible and certainly more vulnerable as their true budgetary costs emerge. This is especially true for the heavily subsidized programs supporting rural housing, rural electrification, and farm exports.

The absence of comprehensiveness in the federal budgetary process has created an imbalance between advocacy committees, such as agriculture, and control committees. In fact, before the budget committees began to develop credit budgets, there were no committees that routinely reviewed the fiscal implications of credit programs. As a result, advocacy within Congress was virtually unchecked, and it was not until the Carter administration's credit budget proposals that credit policy—as opposed to individual programs—received serious attention in Congress. Comprehensiveness requires, however, not just an end to off-budget evasions but also "cost equivalence" between direct spending, tax, and credit programs. Such equivalence would introduce a necessary measure of fiscal reality (and fiscal discipline) into the politics of federal credit.

Budgets as Controls

Integrating the subsidy costs of federal credit activity into the unified budget produces some important benefits. It corrects the competitive imbalance between spending assistance and credit assistance. It allows for reconciliation trade-offs between credit and spending. With visibility heightened and enforcement strengthened for credit programs, major budgetary evasions are less likely than in the past.

"Costing" federal credit also makes it more difficult to ignore programmatic issues such as private market duplication, inappropriate subsidies, and cost-effectiveness. If a federal program can in fact be replaced by private credit, there are budgetary savings to be gained by eliminating it. If subsidies are too large or eligibility too liberal, budgetary savings are again possible through subsidy reductions or targeted assistance.

Credit budget reforms improve the accuracy and comprehensiveness of the unified budget. They leave unresolved, however, the accountability problems associated with government-sponsored enterprises. Although the Congress might occasionally intervene in the operations of these enterprises, there is no sustained oversight of government-sponsored lending by either the executive or legislative branch.[35] Despite protestations to the contrary, government-sponsored enterprises are not independent. They have significant and advantageous links with the government. Most important, they enjoy preferred borrowing status. But while their borrowing and lending activities have increased enormously, there has yet to be any comprehensive congressional examination of the efficacy or desirability of these quasi-governmental bodies.

It is unlikely that the Reagan administration's proposals for full privatization will do much to change Congress's customary passivity regarding government-sponsored enterprises. At the same time, it is futile to assign great weight to credit budgets when massive lending by these organizations is proceeding with little governmental oversight or control. It may well be that the only way to raise the accountability, oversight, and policy issues related to government-sponsored enterprises is through a special commission, much like the ones established by presidents Kennedy and Johnson.

This approach has been endorsed by recent administrations and enjoys some support in Congress. The unresolved question is whether its charge should be limited to credit programs or broadened to cover other budget-control issues. One of the obvious drawbacks to even the most far-reaching credit budget reforms is that they might exacerbate existing problems of spending and deficit control. Placing credit subsidies and spending assistance on a competitive basis, for example, might result in even looser budgets, as popular programs run into budget totals. If the federal budget is out of control, as some critics charge, the additional weight of credit program subsidies will not help.

The ongoing discussions of budget reform in Congress, moreover, are likely to produce at best modest improvements in the operation of the 1974 budget act. That legislation has had a very limited impact on spending control and budget policy, although it has introduced some procedural coherence into congressional budgeting. Without centralized control, neither spending budgets nor credit budgets can ultimately be enforced. Yet centralized fiscal control is hardly likely to emerge from a reform proposal that the Congress initiates.

A special commission on budget control—which would encompass spending, credit, off-budget entities, and government-sponsored enterprises—is perhaps the only forum in which the broad range of procedural, organizational, and budget-accounting weaknesses can be objectively analyzed and a coherent reform package developed. It is almost certainly the best means for promoting complementary reforms in the executive branch and Congress.

Given the remarkably prescient analyses of the 1967 President's Commission on Budget Concepts, along with the nearly two decades of accumulated experience and expertise (and problems) since its report was issued, a successor body would have a solid foundation upon which to work.

Credit budgets are an appealing "good government" reform. They will be a meaningful reform only if they constrain credit programs. The simple and unfortunate fact is that we do not have a budget control mechanism that works for spending. A solution to problems of credit control, therefore, inevitably means substantially strengthened *general* budget control at the federal level.

The case for a credit budget or a spending budget depends upon certain assumptions about fiscal politics in a democracy. It assumes that economic resources are scarce, while beneficent purposes and good intentions are not. It assumes that procedures and organization affect the fiscal responsibility of political institutions. It assumes, finally, that informed policy choices cannot be made without a knowledge of *all* the costs as well as the benefits of government intervention.

Notes

Chapter 1

1. The "official budget" is a unified, cash-flow document that shows the actual cash transactions of the federal government. These transactions, expressed as outlays and budget authority on the spending side, are the bases of the annual presidential budgets and congressional budget resolutions. The bulk of federal credit activity is carried on outside the unified budget.

2. *Special Analysis F, Federal Credit Programs, Budget of the United States Government, Fiscal Year 1984* (Washington, D.C.: Government Printing Office, 1983), p. F-6. This does not include outstanding credit of government-sponsored enterprises, which would bring the total to $765 billion for fiscal 1982.

3. Senate Committee on the Budget, Task Force on Credit, *Statement of Alice M. Rivlin, Director, Congressional Budget Office* (Washington, D.C.: Congressional Budget Office, 10 Dec. 1981), p. 1.

4. Clifford M. Hardin and Arthur T. Denzau, *The Unrestrained Growth of Federal Credit Programs* (St. Louis: Washington University, Center for the Study of American Business, 1981), p. 2.

5. *Special Analysis F, Federal Credit Programs, Budget of the United States Government, Fiscal Year 1983* (Washington, D.C.: Government Printing Office, 1982), p. 6.

6. *Budget of the United States Government, Fiscal Year 1981* (Washington, D.C.: Government Printing Office, 1980), pp. 17–21.

7. *Fiscal Year 1982 Budget Revisions* (Washington, D.C.: Government Printing Office, 1981), p. 17.

8. Bruce K. MacLaury, "Federal Credit Programs—The Issues They Raise," in *Issues in Federal Debt Management, Conference Series no. 10* (Boston: Federal Reserve Bank of Boston, 1973), p. 214.

9. Loan guarantees are excluded from the definitions of budget authority and spending authority contained in sections 3(a)(2) and 401(c)(2) of the Congressional Budget and Impoundment Control Act of 1974. The unified budget also excludes the transactions of agencies referred to as government-sponsored enterprises (see chapter 2).

10. The contingent liability estimate for fiscal year 1983 is $568.8 billion. *Special Analysis F, Fiscal Year 1984*, p. F-9.

11. Congressional Budget Office, *Federal Credit Activities: An Overview of the President's Credit Budget for Fiscal Year 1983* (Washington, D.C.: Congressional Budget Office, 1982), p. 2.

12. The Federal Financing Bank is treated in greater detail in chapter 3.

13. Hardin and Denzau, *The Unrestrained Growth of Federal Credit Programs*, p. 9.

14. See ibid., p. 12, for other means of financing the federal debt that add to the reported budget deficit.

15. Between 1973 and 1982 (including the fiscal 1976–77 transition quarter), outlays of off-budget entities added almost $105 billion to the federal debt. The combined deficits (minus surpluses) for the 1950s and 1960s were less than $75 billion. See *Budget of the United States Government, Fiscal Year 1983* (Washington, D.C.: Government Printing Office, 1982), p. 9-62.

16. Herman B. Leonard and Elisabeth H. Rhyne, "Federal Credit and the 'Shadow Budget,'" *Public Interest* 65 (Fall 1981): 57.

17. See Hardin and Denzau. *The Unrestrained Growth of Federal Credit Programs*, pp. 15–16.

18. Office of Mangement and Budget, Debt Collection Project, *Report on Strengthening Federal Credit Management*, vol. 1 (Washington, D.C.: Office of Management and Budget, 1981), pp. 32–33.

19. Ibid, p. 35.

20. See Hardin and Denzau, *The Unrestrained Growth of Federal Credit Programs*, p. 16. In 1982 Congress finally responded to this problem by exempting credit bureaus from privacy act restrictions as part of legislation designed to help the federal government collect delinquent debts (HR 4613).

21. General Accounting Office, *The Congress Should Control Federal Credit Programs to Promote Economic Stabilization* (Washington, D.C.: General Accounting Office, 21 Oct. 1981), p. iii.

22. *Special Analysis F, Fiscal Year 1983*, p. 50.

23. *Special Analysis F, Federal Credit Programs, Budget of the United States Government, Fiscal Year 1981* (Washington, D.C.: Government Printing Office, 1980), pp. 195–98.

24. *Special Analysis F, Fiscal Year 1984*, pp. F-57–F-58.

25. General Accounting Office, *The Congress Should Control Federal Credit Programs*, pp. 7–11.

26. Congressional Budget Office, *Federal Credit Activities: An Overview of the President's Credit Budget for Fiscal Year 1983*, p. 5.

27. The phrase is Representative Ed Bethune's. Bethune, an Arkansas Republican, is one of a handful of members of Congress who have made serious attempts to improve credit control procedures. He and Norman Mineta (D-Calif.) have provided much of the credit budget leadership on the House Budget Committee. Slade Gorton (R-Wash.) has performed a similar role on the Senate Budget Committee.

Bethune has also described credit issues as "boring" and "arcane," lamenting that there are "no villains, no heroes, no sordid stories, impending catastrophes. What we need is a little sex appeal on this issue here." See House Budget Committee, Task Force on Enforcement, Credit, and Multiyear Budgeting, *Hearing, Fiscal Year 1983 Credit Budget* (Washington, D.C.: Government Printing Office, 12 Mar. 1982), p. 22.

Chapter 2

1. Fiscal 1921 outlays were $5.1 billion, compared to $3.1 billion in fiscal 1929. Over this period, budget surpluses totaled $7.3 billion, which was almost one-fourth of total spending. *Budget of the United States Government, Fiscal Year 1983* (Washington, D.C.: Government Printing Office, 1982), p. 9-62.

2. U.S. Bureau of the Census, *Historical Statistics of the United States, Colonial Times to 1970, Part 2* (Washington: D.C.: Government Printing Office, 1975), p. 1116.

3. The health and income security functions discussed below include medicare and social security, respectively. The Social Security Act Amendments of 1983 (P.L. 98-21) separated social security from other income security programs and medicare (medical insurance) from other health outlays. The broader, pre-1983 functions are used here to facilitate historical comparisons of spending patterns.

4. Measured in constant (fiscal year 1972) prices; *Budget of the United States Government, Fiscal Year 1983*, p. 9-61.

5. House Committee on the Budget, Task Force on Budget Process, *Hearings, Control of Federal Credit Programs* (Washington, D.C.: Government Printing Office, 13 and 14 Nov. 1979), p. 4.

6. The use of off-budget direct lending has reduced this ratio in recent years. See Congressional Budget Office, *Loan Guarantees: Current Concerns and Alternatives for Control* (Washington: D.C.: Congressional Budget Office, 1978), pp. 4–5.

7. Ibid., p. 11.

8. A 1977 Congressional Research Service study examined fifty-nine loan guarantee programs for which continuous data were available over a sixteen-year period. Of these, thirty-seven were categorized as programs for marginal borrowers, compared to four actuarially sound programs. See ibid., pp. 11–12.

9. For an examination of default problems, see Office of Management and Budget, Debt Collection Project, *Report on Strengthening Federal Credit Management* (Washington, D.C.: Office of Management and Budget, 1981).

10. This was the case with education benefits for veterans after World War II and Korea.

11. *Budget of the United States Government, Fiscal Year 1984* (Washington, D.C.: Government Printing Office, 1983), p. 5-86.

12. This ceiling was set in 1980. Previously it had been 7 percent. There have been recent efforts to raise the ceiling, but Congress has rejected these, along with other major changes in the student loan program.

13. *Budget of the United States Government, Fiscal Year 1984*, p. 5-86.

14. *Congressional Record* 128 (13 May 1982): S5039.

15. See *Congressional Quarterly Weekly Report* 40 (22 May 1982): 1167–72.

16. Congressional Budget Office, *Loan Guarantees: Current Concerns and Alternatives for Control* (Washington, D.C.: Congressional Budget Office, 1979), p. 217.

17. Congressional Budget Office, *Loan Guarantees* (1978), p. 14.

18. *Special Analysis F, Federal Credit Programs, Budget of the United States Government, Fiscal Year 1984* (Washington, D.C.: Government Printing Office, 1983), pp. F-35–F-36.

19. Senate Committee on the Budget, Staff Report of the Task Force on Energy, *Federal Energy Financing* (Washington, D.C.: Government Printing Office, 30 Aug. 1976), p. 1.

20. Robert D. Reischauer, "The Federal Budget: Subsidies for the Rich," in *The Federal Budget: Economics and Politics*, ed. M. J. Boskin and A. Wildavsky (San Francisco: Institute for Contemporary Studies, 1982), pp. 253–55.

21. Some go back even further. The Reclamation Act of 1902 created a fund to support interest-free loans for construction of irrigation water projects. The initial

payback schedule of ten years was extended to twenty years in 1914, to forty years in 1926, and to fifty years in 1939.

22. Data for the period 1950–77 are available in Congressional Budget Office, *Loan Guarantees* (1979), pp. 32–35. Data for subsequent years are carried in *Special Analyses, Federal Credit Programs, Budget of the United States Government.*

23. Robert J. Samuelson, "Administration Slips and Stumbles in Efforts to Cut Off-Budget Spending," *National Journal* 31 (13 June 1981): 1071.

24. See *Congressional Quarterly Almanac, 1973* (Washington, D.C.: Congressional Quarterly, Inc., 1974), pp. 316–17.

25. The "debudgeting" of the REA also spurred a dramatic increase in the use of loan guarantees. These had not been used prior to 1973 but had reached $15.5 billion in outstanding guarantees by the end of fiscal 1981.

26. Samuelson, "Administration Slips and Stumbles," p. 1071.

27. *Congressional Quarterly Almanac, 1981* (Washington, D.C.: Congressional Quarterly, Inc., 1982), p. 123.

28. Samuelson, "Administration Slips and Stumbles," p. 1069.

29. Herman B. Leonard and Elisabeth H. Rhyne, "Federal Credit and the 'Shadow Budget,'" *Public Interest* 65 (Fall 1981): 57.

30. *Special Analysis F, Fiscal Year 1984*, p. F-53.

31. Rochelle L. Stanfield, "States, Cities Can't Agree on the Need for Tax-Exempt Development Bonds," *National Journal* 14 (15 May 1982): 871.

32. Ibid.; *Special Analysis F, Fiscal Year 1983*, p. 47.

33. The single largest user of industrial revenue bonds is the K Mart Corp., the nation's second largest retailer. Stanfield, "States, Cities Can't Agree on the Need for Tax-Exempt Development Bonds," p. 871.

34. *Special Analysis F, Fiscal Year 1984*, p. F-53.

35. Ibid.

Chapter 3

1. Statement of Harry S. Havens, Assistant Comptroller General, U.S. General Accounting Office, in Senate Committee on the Budget, *Hearings, Control of Federal Credit* (Washington, D.C.: Government Printing Office, 1980), p. 82.

2. Ibid.

3. Herman B. Leonard and Elisabeth H. Rhyne, "Federal Credit and the 'Shadow Budget,'" *Public Interest* 65 (Fall 1981): 58.

4. See Congressional Budget Office, *Loan Guarantees: Current Concerns and Alternatives for Control* (Washington, D.C.: Congressional Budget Office, 1979), p. 14.

5. This discussion is drawn from Congressional Budget Office, *The Federal Financing Bank and the Budgetary Treatment of Federal Credit Activities* (Washington, D.C.: Congressional Budget Office, 1982), pp. 15–20.

6. Trust funds are monies earmarked when collected for specific purposes and are not available for the general purposes of government. Examples include the social security and unemployment compensation trust funds. General funds are monies not earmarked at their source. These, along with borrowing, are used to support general governmental functions.

7. President's Commission on Budget Concepts, *Report* (Washington, D.C.: Government Printing Office, 1967), p. 47.

8. President's Committee on Federal Credit Programs, *Report* (Washington, D.C.: Government Printing Office, 1963), p. 33.

9. Ibid.

10. The debt limit issue arose because FNMA securities used for the participation certificate sales would, unlike Treasury securities, not be subject to the public debt limit.

11. Quoted in Congressional Budget Office, *Loan Guarantees* (1979), p. 88.

12. Ibid., p. 89.

13. Quoted in President's Commission on Budget Concepts, *Staff Papers and Other Materials Reviewed by the President's Commission* (Washington, D.C.: Government Printing Office, 1967), p. 293.

14. Ibid.

15. President's Commission on Budget Concepts, *Report*, p. 55.

16. Ibid.

17. President's Commission on Budget Concepts, *Staff Papers*, p. 292.

18. Quoted in Congressional Budget Office, *Loan Guarantees* (1979), p. 91. The bank was moved back on budget in fiscal 1977.

19. *United States Statutes at Large* (Washington, D.C.: Government Printing Office, 1976), 88:1832.

20. President's Commission on Budget Concepts, *Report*, p. 49.

21. Ibid., p. 50.

22. See Congressional Budget Office, *Loan Guarantees: Current Concerns and Alternatives for Control* (Washington, D.C.: Congressional Budget Office, 1978), p. 30.

23. Under Sec. 3(a)(2), "The term 'budget authority' means authority provided by law to enter into obligations which will result in immediate or future outlays involving Government funds, except that such term does not include authority to insure or guarantee the repayment of indebtedness incurred by another person or government." See Senate Committee on the Budget, *Congressional Budget and Impoundment Control Act of 1974, As Amended* (Washington, D.C.: Government Printing Office, 1983), p. 3.

24. Senate Committee on Rules and Administration, *Report No. 93-688, Congressional Budget Act of 1974* (Washington, D.C.: Government Printing Office, 1974), p. 13.

25. *Congressional Record* 120 (18 June 1974): 19697.

26. *United States Statutes at Large* (Washington, D.C.: Government Printing Office, 1974), 87:937.

27. Department of the Treasury, *Report of the Secretary of the Treasury, 1972* (Washington, D.C.: Government Printing Office, 1973), p. 273.

28. Congressional Budget Office, *The Federal Financing Bank*, p. 5.

29. House Committee on Ways and Means, *Hearings, Federal Financing Bank Act* (Washington, D.C.: Government Printing Office, 1973), p. 15.

30. House Committee on Ways and Means, *Hearings, Federal Financing Bank Act* (Washington, D.C.: Government Printing Office, 1972), p. 20.

31. Congressional Budget Office, *Federal Financing Bank*, p. 13.

32. *President's Message to Congress on the Fiscal 1969 Budget*, in *Congressional*

Quarterly Almanac, 1968 (Washington, D.C.: Congressional Quarterly, Inc., 1968), p. 20-A.

33. See *Budget of the United States Government, Fiscal Year 1983* (Washington, D.C.: Government Printing Office, 1982), p. 9-5.

34. Ibid., pp. 9-50–9-56.

Chapter 4

1. *Budget of the United States Government, Fiscal Year 1972* (Washington, D.C.: Government Printing Office, 1971), p. 17.

2. Ibid., p. 18.

3. See chapter 3.

4. President's Commission on Budget Concepts, *Report* (Washington, D.C.: Government Printing Office, 1967), p. 30.

5. Ibid., p. 25. The commission also recommended, however, that transactions of the government-sponsored enterprises be "included at a prominent place in the budget as a memorandum item."

6. The Environmental Financing Authority was created in 1972 as an off-budget agency to purchase obligations of state and local agencies used to finance the non-federal share of waste treatment works. Initial capital of $100 million was provided, and the authority was authorized to borrow an addition $200 million from the Treasury. Administrative delays prevented substantial program activity before the authority's authorization expired in 1975.

7. See Stephen H. Pollock, "Off-Budget Federal Outlays," *Economic Review, Federal Reserve Bank of Kansas City* 66 (Mar. 1981): 14–15.

8. The off-budget status was rescinded in 1974 effective for the fiscal 1977 budget.

9. Senate Committee on Banking and Currency, *Report No. 91-1462, Amending the Export-Import Bank Act of 1945, As Amended, To Allow For Greater Expansion of U.S. Export Trade* (Washington, D.C.: Government Printing Office, 1970), p. 2.

10. Ibid., p. 3.

11. Ibid.

12. Quoted in *Congressional Quarterly Weekly Report* 29 (12 Mar. 1971): 563.

13. Presidential estimates for fiscal years 1971–76 ranged from $3.6 to $7.6 billion. Congressional program activity limits matched these in fiscal years 1971 and 1974, while continuing resolutions were necessary for the broader appropriation bill in the other fiscal years.

14. Congressional Budget Office, *The Export-Import Bank: Implications for the Federal Budget and the Credit Market* (Washington, D.C.: Congressional Budget Office, 27 Oct. 1976), p. ix.

15. Richard E. Feinberg, *Subsidizing Success: The Export-Import Bank in the U.S. Economy* (Cambridge: Cambridge University Press, 1982), pp. 136–37.

16. Ibid., pp. 91–96. See also John H. Boyd, "Eximbank Lending: A Federal Program That Costs Too Much," *Federal Reserve Bank of Minneapolis Quarterly Review* (Winter 1982), pp. 1–17.

17. *Special Analysis F, Federal Credit Programs, Budget of the United States Government, Fiscal Year 1984* (Washington, D.C.: Government Printing Office, 1983), p. F-58.

18. Congressional Budget Office, *The Export-Import Bank*, pp. 16–17.

19. *Congressional Quarterly Weekly Report* 39 (11 July 1981): 1247.

20. *Special Analysis F, Fiscal Year 1984*, p. F-36.

21. *Budget of the United States Government, Fiscal Year 1984, Appendix* (Washington, D.C.: Government Printing Office, 1983), p. 165.

22. *United States Statutes at Large* (Washington, D.C.: Government Printing Office, 1974), 87:68.

23. It also contained provisions for 2 percent loans in special cases.

24. *Special Analysis F, Fiscal Year 1984*, p. F-57.

25. *United States Statutes at Large* (Washington, D.C.: Government Printing Office, 1981), 94:669.

26. Ibid., p. 649.

27. *Budget of the United States Government, Fiscal Year 1984* (Washington, D.C.: Government Printing Office, 1983), p. 5-37.

28. This is included in the budget under the commerce and housing credit function.

29. House Committee on the Budget, *Report No. 94-1740, Off-Budget Activities of the Federal Government* (Washington, D.C.: Government Printing Office, 1976), p. 11.

30. House Committee on the Budget, *Report No. 95-1055, First Concurrent Resolution on the Budget—Fiscal Year 1979* (Washington, D.C.: Government Printing Office, 14 April 1978), p. 23.

31. See House Committee on the Budget, *Report No. 94-1740*, pp. 6–7.

32. House Committee on the Budget, *Hearings, Federal Credit Activity and H.R. 2372* (Washington, D.C.: Government Printing Office, 28–29 Oct. 1981), p. 28.

33. Congressional Budget Office, *Loan Guarantees: Current Concerns and Alternatives for Control* (Washington, D.C.: Congressional Budget Office, 1978), p. 26.

34. *Congressional Quarterly Almanac, 1970* (Washington, D.C.: Congressional Quarterly, Inc., 1971), p. 810.

35. *United States Statutes at Large* (Washington, D.C.: Government Printing Office, 1971), 84:1975.

36. Robert J. Samuelson, "The High Cost of Bailouts," *National Journal* 15 (28 May 1983): 1126.

37. Senate Committee on Banking, Housing and Urban Affairs, *Hearings, Emergency Loan Guarantee Legislation* (Washington, D.C.: Government Printing Office, 7–16 June 1971), p. 19.

38. Ibid., p. 10.

39. Ibid., p. 19.

40. Ibid.

41. House Committee on Banking and Currency, *Hearings, To Authorize Emergency Loan Guarantees to Major Business Enterprises* (Washington, D.C.: Government Printing Office, 13–20 July 1971), p. 293.

42. Ibid.

43. Ibid.

44. Senate Committee on Banking, Housing and Urban Affairs, *Report No. 92-270, Emergency Loan Guarantees to Major Business Enterprises* (Washington, D.C.: Government Printing Office, 1971), p. 3.

45. Ibid., p. 17.

46. *United States Statutes at Large* (Washington, D.C.: Government Printing Office, 1972), 85:178.

47. *United States Statutes at Large* (Washington, D.C.: Government Printing Office, 1980), 92:462.

48. Ibid.

49. *Congressional Record* 125 (18 Dec. 1979): 36840.

50. Ibid., p. 36777. Stockman was the only member of the Michigan delegation to vote against the Chrysler loan guarantee legislation.

51. *United States Statutes at Large* (Washington, D.C.: Government Printing Office, 1981), 93:1326.

52. Ibid., p. 1335.

53. Ibid., p. 1319.

54. *Congressional Record* 125 (20 Dec. 1979): 37206–11.

55. Ibid., p. 37211.

56. On the issue of budget reform spending bias, see Louis Fisher, "The Congressional Budget Act: Does It Have a Spending Bias," paper presented to the Conference on the Congressional Budget Process, Carl Albert Congressional Research and Studies Center, University of Oklahoma, Norman, 12–13 Feb. 1982.

Chapter 5

1. See, for example, House Committee on the Budget, Task Force on Budget Process, *Hearings, Control of Federal Credit Programs* (Washington, D.C.: Government Printing Office, 13–14 Nov. 1979); Senate Committee on the Budget, Special Subcommittee on Control of Federal Credit, *Hearings, Control of Federal Credit* (Washington, D.C.: Government Printing Office, 19, 23 June and 1 July 1980).

2. Congressional Budget Office, *An Analysis of the President's Budgetary Proposals for Fiscal Year 1981* (Washington, D.C.: Congressional Budget Office, Feb. 1980), p. 51.

3. House Committee on the Budget, *Report No. 95-1055, First Concurrent Resolution on the Budget—Fiscal Year 1979* (Washington, D.C.: Government Printing Office, 14 April 1978), p. 162.

4. *Budget of the United States Government, Fiscal Year 1978* (Washington, D.C.: Government Printing Office, 1977), p. 33.

5. For a parallel argument about process versus policy with regard to spending, see Dennis S. Ippolito, *Congressional Spending* (Ithaca: Cornell University Press, 1981), pp. 244–46.

6. *Budget of the United States Government, Fiscal Year 1978*, p. 29. Office of Management and Budget, *Issues '78, Perspectives on Fiscal Year 1978 Budget* (Washington, D.C.: Government Printing Office, 1977), pp. 236–37.

7. *Issues '78*, pp. 238–39.

8. Ibid., p. 238.

9. *Budget of the United States Government, Fiscal Year 1979* (Washington, D.C.: Government Printing Office, 1978), p. 27.

10. Ibid.

11. Ibid., pp. 25–26.

12. Ibid., p. 26.

13. *Budget of the United States Government, Fiscal Year 1981* (Washington, D.C.: Government Printing Office, 1980), p. 17.

14. *United States Statutes at Large* (Washington, D.C.: Government Printing Office, 1976), 88:306.

15. *Special Analysis F, Federal Credit Programs, Budget of the United States Government, Fiscal Year 1981* (Washington, D.C.: Government Printing Office, 1980), p. 202.

16. House Committee on the Budget, *Hearings, Economic Issues for Fiscal Year 1981, Part I* (Washington, D.C.: Government Printing Office, 1980), p. 432.

17. Congressional Budget Office, *Federal Credit Activities: An Analysis of the President's Credit Budget for 1981* (Washington, D.C.: Congressional Budget Office, February 1980), p. 14.

18. Ibid., p. 11.

19. The second resolution for fiscal 1981, which was adopted on 20 November 1980, raised the spending ceiling by $20 billion and projected a $27 billion deficit. The revised second resolution, which was adopted the following May, raised the spending ceiling an additional $30 billion and projected a $58 billion deficit.

20. See Ippolito, *Congressional Spending*, pp. 40–53.

21. House Committee on the Budget, *Report No. 96-857, First Concurrent Resolution on the Budget—Fiscal Year 1981* (Washington, D.C.: Government Printing Office, 1980), p. 19.

22. Ibid.

23. Ibid.

24. The Senate Budget Committee characterized the president's proposals as "a limited first step" and found the limitations of the appropriations process "incomplete." The committee stated that "the president's proposed credit control system does not fully control the fastest growing sectors of Federal credit activity—loan guarantees and direct lending by the FFB, the largest off-budget agency." Senate Committee on the Budget, *Report No. 96-654, First Concurrent Resolution on the Budget FY 1981* (Washington, D.C.: Government Printing Office, 1980), p. 257.

25. House Committee on the Budget, *First Concurrent Resolution on the Budget—Fiscal Year 1981*, p. 20.

26. Senate Committee on the Budget, *First Concurrent Resolution on the Budget FY 1981*, p. 20.

27. House Committee on the Budget, *Report No. 96-1463, Second Concurrent Resolution on the Budget—Fiscal Year 1981* (Washington, D.C.: Government Printing Office, 1980), p. 31.

28. *United States Statutes at Large* (Washington, D.C.: Government Printing Office, 1981), 94:3045.

29. Ibid., p. 3048.

30. Ibid., p. 3046.

31. Ibid., p. 3105.

32. Ibid., p. 3104.

33. Ibid., p. 3107.

34. Ibid., p. 3117.

35. *Special Analysis F, Fiscal Year 1981*, p. 202; *Special Analysis F, Federal*

Credit Programs, Budget of the United States Government, Fiscal Year 1982 (Washington, D.C.: Government Printing Office, 1981), p. 196.

36. *Budget of the United States Government, Fiscal Year 1982* (Washington, D.C.: Government Printing Office, 1981), p. M12.

37. Ibid., pp. M12–M13.

38. Ibid., p. 20.

Chapter 6

1. *Fiscal Year 1982 Budget Revisions* (Washington, D.C.: Government Printing Office, March 1981), p. 17.

2. *Budget of the United States Government, Fiscal Year 1984* (Washington, D.C.: Government Printing Office, 1983), p. 9-54.

3. Excluding, of course, the fiscal 1981 budgets. These are not comparable, given the almost one-year gap between enactment of the first fiscal 1981 congressional budget resolution and President Reagan's fiscal 1981 revisions.

4. See Congressional Budget Office, *An Analysis of the President's Credit Budget for Fiscal Year 1984* (Washington, D.C.: Congressional Budget Office, March 1983), p. 27.

5. *Special Analysis F, Federal Credit Programs, Budget of the United States Government, Fiscal Year 1984* (Washington, D.C.: Government Printing Office, 1983), p. F-4.

6. Elisabeth H. Rhyne, "Federal Credit Activities," in *Setting National Priorities: The 1984 Budget*, ed. J. A. Pechman (Washington, D.C.: Brookings Institution, 1983), p. 235.

7. *Weekly Compilation of Presidential Documents* (Washington, D.C.: Government Printing Office, 1981), 17:1027.

8. Senate Committee on the Budget, Temporary Task Force on Federal Credit, *Hearings, Overview of Federal Credit* (Washington, D.C.: Government Printing Office, 1982), pp. 581–91.

9. *United States Statutes at Large* (Washington, D.C.: Government Printing Office, 1982), 95:958, 959. None of the regular appropriations bills had been enacted when fiscal year 1982 began.

10. Ibid., p. 1200.

11. Senate Committee on the Budget, *Hearings, Overview of Federal Credit*, p. 338.

12. Ibid., pp. 338–39.

13. Congressional Budget Office, *Federal Credit Activities: An Overview of the President's Credit Budget for Fiscal Year 1983* (Washington, D.C.: Congressional Budget Office, March 1982), p. 23.

14. Congressional Budget Office, *An Analysis of the President's Credit Budget for Fiscal Year 1984*, p. ix.

15. Ibid., p. 17.

16. *Special Analysis F, Fiscal Year 1984*, p. F-61.

17. Ibid., p. F-40.

18. Congressional Budget Office, *An Analysis of the President's Credit Budget for Fiscal Year 1984*, pp. 21, 72.

19. Ibid., p. 96.

20. Executive Office of the President, Office of Management and Budget, *Statement of Lawrence A. Kudlow before the Senate Budget Committee Task Force on Federal Credit* (Washington, D.C.: Office of Management and Budget, 22 June 1982), p. 9.

21. Congressional Budget Office, *An Analysis of the President's Credit Budget for Fiscal Year 1984*, p. 14.

22. Ibid., pp. 14–20.

23. Spending as a share of GNP for fiscal 1983 is estimated at 25.7 percent (including off-budget outlays), the highest in several decades. The fiscal 1984 budget calls for reducing this to 24.1 percent by fiscal 1986. *Budget of the United States Government, Fiscal Year 1984*, p. 9-53. President Reagan had initially hoped to reduce the spending share of GNP to 19.3 percent by fiscal 1984. See *Fiscal Year 1982 Budget Revisions*, p. 6.

24. Congressional Budget Office, *An Analysis of the President's Credit Budget for Fiscal Year 1984*, p. 23.

25. Senate Committee on the Budget, *Report No. 97-478, First Concurrent Resolution on the Budget—Fiscal Year 1983* (Washington, D.C.: Government Printing Office, 1982), p. 15.

26. Ibid., p. 16.

27. *United States Statutes at Large* (Washington, D.C.: Government Printing Office, 1976), 88:317. The more stringent requirement that credit become available only to the extent provided in appropriation acts created a parliamentary obstacle when the House considered emergency credit legislation in 1983. The potential point-of-order enforcement was set aside when the House adopted a special rule governing debate on the bill.

28. *Congressional Record* 128 (23 June 1982): S7339.

29. House Committee on Appropriations, *Report No. 97-669, Subdivision of Budget Totals for Fiscal Years 1982 and 1983 and Credit Activity Totals for Fiscal Year 1983* (Washington, D.C.: Government Printing Office, 1982), p. 2.

30. Ibid.

31. Senate Committee on the Budget, *First Concurrent Resolution on the Budget, Fiscal Year 1983*, p. 32.

32. *Congressional Record* 128 (23 June 1982): S7339.

33. Ibid., p. S7340.

34. See Congressional Budget Office estimates reported in *Congressional Quarterly Weekly Report* 40 (23 Oct. 1982): 2722.

35. Senate Committee on the Budget, *Report No. 98-155, First Concurrent Resolution on the Budget—Fiscal Year 1984* (Washington, D.C.: Government Printing Office, 1983), p. 25.

36. Ibid., p. 27.

37. Congressional Budget Office, *An Analysis of the President's Credit Budget for Fiscal Year 1984*, pp. 11–12.

38. Ibid., p. 46.

39. See *Congressional Record* 128 (18 Aug. 1982): H6395; (23 Sept. 1982): H7542.

40. See *Congressional Record* 128 (18 Aug. 1982): H6376.

41. Ibid., p. 6395.

42. *Congressional Record* (23 Sept. 1982): H7542.

43. Ibid.

44. *Congressional Quarterly Weekly Report* 41 (6 Aug. 1983): 1605.

Chapter 7

1. Edward J. Kane, "Deposit-Interest Ceilings and Sectoral Shortages of Credit: How to Improve Credit Allocation without Allocating Credit," in *Government Credit Allocation* (San Francisco: Institute for Contemporary Studies, 1975), pp. 15–16.

2. For other distortions, see Statement of Charles A. Bowsher, Comptroller General of the United States, Senate Committee on the Budget, *Hearings, Proposed Improvements in the Congressional Budget Act of 1974* (Washington, D.C.: Government Printing Office, 1982), pp. 164–66.

3. For an examination of evasions by state and local governments, see James T. Bennett and Thomas J. DiLorenzo, *Underground Government: The Off-Budget Public Sector* (Washington, D.C.: Cato Institute, 1983).

4. See Congressional Budget Office, *Conference on the Economics of Federal Credit Activity, Part 1, Proceedings* (Washington, D.C.: Congressional Budget Office, 1980).

5. See *Government Credit Allocation*, chapters 1–4.

6. Aaron Wildavsky, *The Politics of the Budgetary Process* (Boston: Little, Brown, 1964), p. 132.

7. Interviews with staff members of the House and Senate budget committees, 6–7 Dec. 1982.

8. It is also possible to delay enrollment of spending bills until all spending legislation has passed, but Congress has not used this procedure.

9. Alice M. Rivlin and Robert W. Hartman, "Control of Federal Credit under the Congressional Budget Process," paper prepared for the Conference Board, Toward a Reconstruction of Federal Budgeting, Washington, D.C., 2 Dec. 1982, p. 4.

10. Allen Schick, *Reconciliation and the Congressional Budget Process* (Washington, D.C.: American Enterprise Institute, 1981).

11. This is the language used in concurrent budget resolutions.

12. *Special Analysis B, Federal Transactions in the National Income Accounts, Budget of the United States Government, Fiscal Year 1984* (Washington, D.C.: Government Printing Office, 1983), p. B-1.

13. Dennis S. Ippolito, *Congressional Spending* (Ithaca: Cornell University Press, 1981), pp. 90–95.

14. Dennis S. Ippolito, "Congressional Budgets and Fiscal Policy," in *The United States Congress*, ed. D. Hale (Boston: Boston College, 1982), pp. 135–53.

15. *Congressional Record*, 127 (16 Nov. 1981): S13391.

16. See Rivlin and Hartman, "Control of Federal Credit under the Congressional Budget Process," p. 7.

17. Elisabeth H. Rhyne, "Federal Credit Activities," in *Setting National Priorities: The 1984 Budget*, ed. J. A. Pechman (Washington, D.C.: Brookings Institution, 1983), p. 236.

18. Ibid., p. 235.

19. Ippolito, *Congressional Spending*, p. 136.

20. Rivlin and Hartman, "Control of Federal Credit under the Congressional Budget Process," p. 26.

21. See President's Commission on Budget Concepts, *Staff Papers and Other Materials Reviewed by the President's Commission* (Washington, D.C.: Government Printing Office, 1967), p. 301.

22. Ibid.

23. Ibid.

24. President's Commission on Budget Concepts, *Report* (Washington, D.C.: Government Printing Office, 1967), p. 47.

25. Ibid.

26. Rivlin and Hartman, "Control of Federal Credit under the Congressional Budget Process," p. 22.

27. See *Special Analysis F, Federal Credit Programs, Budget of the United States Government, Fiscal Year 1982* (Washington, D.C.: Government Printing Office, 1981), p. 193.

28. Office of Management and Budget, Debt Collection Project, *Report on Strengthening Federal Credit Management*, vol. 1 (Washington, D.C.: Office of Management and Budget, 1981).

29. Rhyne, "Federal Credit Activities," p. 242.

30. Office of Management and Budget, *Report on Strengthening Federal Credit Management*.

31. Statement of Alice M. Rivlin, Director, Congressional Budget Office, Senate Committee on the Budget, Temporary Task Force on Federal Credit, *Hearings, Overview of Federal Credit* (Washington, D.C.: Government Printing Office, 1982), pp. 57–58.

32. Ibid., p. 57.

33. Aaron Wildavsky, *The Politics of the Budgetary Process*, 4th ed. (Boston: Little, Brown, 1984), pp. xix–xx.

34. Ibid., p. xx.

35. As examples, Congress has recently extended from three years to ten years the period over which the FNMA can carry back net operating losses and forced the FHLMC to delay a ban on mortgage assumptions of low-interest loans. See Public Laws 97-320, 97-362. As noted in chapter 6, congressional committees have also initiated recapitalization and expansion proposals for government-sponsored enterprises.

Index

Accounting procedures: for federal credit activity, 7–9, 43–64 passim, 76, 115, 120, 129, 130, 135, 138

Agriculture, 94, 101, 110, 145; as focus of federal credit assistance, 3, 16, 18, 23, 65; in spending budget, 18, 20, 23; loan guarantees for, 23, 35–36; and government-sponsored enterprises, 38, 39; "bailout" credit for, 78

Agriculture Department, 36, 73

Amtrak (National Railroad Passenger Corporation), 34, 79, 80, 128

Banks for Cooperatives, 67

Basic Educational Opportunity (Pell) grants, 31, 33

Bauman, Robert, 87

Bethune, Ed, 122, 127, 131, 150 (n. 27)

Boeing Corporation, 37, 72

Bonds. *See* Tax-exempt bonds

Bonior, David E., 127

Bonneville Power Administration, 128

Borrowers, marginal: credit assistance for, 15, 26, 29–33, 34, 42, 139, 151 (n. 8)

Budget, federal: growth of, 3; and credit control, 3, 19, 64–65, 88–89, 90, 131–38; integration of credit into, 3, 37, 69, 138–39, 142; inaccurate reflection of credit activity in, 4, 5, 9–10, 19, 23–26, 37, 43, 46, 50–51, 62, 64, 65–77, 88, 92, 129, 130, 135, 138, 149 (nn. 1, 9); nature and function of, 18, 19, 46, 61, 149 (n. 1); priorities in, 19, 24–26, 56, 58, 61–63; accounting procedures for credit in, 43–44, 45, 61–63, 138–39; and loan asset sales, 45, 46, 49–50; and FFB, 51, 56, 58–60, 61–63; and government-sponsored enterprises, 65–68, 149 (n. 9), 154 (n. 5); credit budget as part of, 106, 131–38; and Reagan administration, 106–19 passim; uncertain future of, 132. *See also* Accounting procedures; Credit assistance; Credit budget; Credit control; Deficit(s); Spending

Carter administration, 3, 74, 84, 86–87, 90–96, 98, 102–4, 145, 157 (n. 24)

Certificates of beneficial interest, 47, 49

Certificates of beneficial ownership, 47, 49–50, 56–58, 61, 62, 63, 74, 92, 101, 125, 135

Certificates of participation, 47–49, 153 (n. 10)

Chrysler Corporation, 34, 65, 77, 85–88, 130, 156 (n. 50)

Committee on Federal Credit Programs (Kennedy administration), 48, 140

Commodity Credit Corporation (CCC), 36, 47, 101, 123

Congress: and credit control, 3, 41, 53, 64, 88–89, 90, 91, 96, 98, 104, 107, 121, 130, 134–37, 144, 145, 150 (n. 27), 161 (n. 35); and off-budget status of credit programs, 10, 37, 92; and politics of credit assistance, 10, 137–38; and overall budget reform, 16, 88–89, 146; and spending control, 19, 24, 97–98, 107, 120, 132–33, 137; spending priorities of, 23, 120; and student loans, 30–33, 151 (n. 12); and REA, 36, 72–75; and deficit reduction, 41, 97–98; and loan asset sales, 48; and FFB, 51, 53–54, 63; and Eximbank, 69–72; and "bailout" credit, 78–80; and development of credit budget, 90, 91, 120–26, 131–34; and Carter credit control system, 98–101, 104; and Reagan credit policy, 106–20 passim, 123, 135; and government-sponsored enterprises, 145–46. *See also* House of Representatives; Senate

Congressional Budget and Impoundment Control Act (1974), 50, 132, 136, 146, 149 (n. 9)

Congressional Budget Office, 5–7, 71, 72, 90, 95, 97, 114, 115, 126, 139

Congressional Research Service, 151 (n. 8)

Connally, John, 81

Conrail (Consolidated Rail Corporation), 34, 80

Credit assistance: growth of, 3, 4, 5–9, 10–11, 17, 18–19, 41–42, 65, 88, 89, 95, 118, 126–28, 130, 142–44; integration of into unified budget, 3, 46, 138–42, 145, 146; and Carter administration, 3, 95, 105; compared with direct spending, 3–4, 5, 11–12, 42, 44, 105, 118, 130, 138–42, 145, 146; inaccurate reflection of in budget, 4, 9, 23–26, 43, 64, 72, 129, 149 (n. 1); subsidies in, 4, 13–15, 105, 138, 144–45; illusory costlessness of, 4, 42, 43, 65, 72, 130, 139, 142–43, 144, 145; defaults on, 7, 13–15; assessing costs of, 11–15, 16, 44, 64, 105, 129, 138, 139, 144–45; economic effects of, 15–16, 64, 105, 118–19, 138, 144; politics of, 16, 17, 24, 63, 88, 101, 142–44; accountability for, 17; and spending control, 19, 88–89, 121, 125–26; as alternative to direct spending, 24, 42, 43, 65, 128, 142–43, 145; accounting procedures for, 43–44, 64, 105, 120, 130, 138, 144; and Congress, 64, 88–89, 105, 109–10, 112–14, 120, 121, 123, 125–28, 130; and Ford administration, 105; and Reagan administration, 106, 109, 112–18, 123, 128; misestimation of in credit budget, 109–10, 126; and budget deficits, 119; justification for, 130, 143, 144; opposition to, 143–44

Credit budget: introduction of, 3, 11, 130; of Carter administration, 3, 145; and costs of federal credit activity, 11, 138; compared with spending budget, 19, 23–26, 95, 102, 107–9, 114, 128, 129, 131, 133; priorities in, 23–26; and government-sponsored enterprises, 40, 146; and credit control, 90–105 passim, 128, 129, 138, 142, 147; appropriations targets or limits in, 98–101, 102, 107, 114, 122–23, 125, 126, 128, 133, 136–38, 142, 157 (n. 24); and credit policy, 102–3, 145; role of in budget process, 106, 107, 120–26, 128, 131–32, 134–38; of Reagan administration, 108–19 passim; misestimation of credit activity in, 109–10; of Congress, 120–26, 128, 144; objective of, 144; rationale for, 147

Credit control: and Ford and Carter administrations, 3, 90–96, 98, 157 (n. 24); and Congress, 3, 98–101, 104, 121, 126, 134–36, 150 (n. 27), 157 (n. 24); and Reagan administration, 3, 106–19, 128, 129; and credit policy, 17, 64, 88, 90, 91–93, 96, 101, 102–3, 106, 107, 114, 120, 129; and FFB, 52; and overall budget reform, 64–65, 129, 147; need for, 89, 90, 131; and development of credit budget, 90–105 passim, 126, 128, 129, 138, 147; and government-sponsored enterprises, 91; and spending control, 92, 105, 132–34; and credit reductions, 95–96; mechanisms for, 134–36; and subsidies, 138, 142

Credit policy: absence or ad hoc nature of, 17, 41–42, 64, 65, 84–85, 87–88, 126; and FFB, 51; and credit budget and credit control, 64, 89, 90, 91–93, 96, 101, 102–3, 106, 107, 109–10, 114, 120, 130, 145; Ford and Carter ambiguity over, 90, 91–93, 96, 102–3; Reagan agenda for, 91, 114–19

Credit supply and demand: effect of federal credit activity on, 4–5, 13–15, 26, 39–40, 41, 130–31; and credit budget, 109, 114, 115

Default(s): and costs of credit assistance, 4, 12, 33, 138–39, 141–42; budgetary treatment of, 7, 9, 107, 138–39, 141–42; rate of in federal credit programs, 7, 12, 29, 33, 78, 103–4
Defense Base Revitalization Act (1982; proposed), 126–27
Defense Department, 58–60, 81–82
Defense Production Act (1950), 126–27
Defense Production Act (1970), 78
Deficit(s): growth of, 3, 9–10, 16, 121; concern over control or reduction of, 3, 10, 41, 91, 97–98, 105, 110, 138, 146; and federal credit activity, 4, 7, 9–10, 150 (n. 15); interest payments on, 16, 20, 23; and FFB, 56, 58–60, 61–63; as reflected in unified budget, 61, 119, 121, 131, 135, 142
Democrats: and "bailout" credit, 79, 82, 83–84, 85, 86; and spending control, 97, 124; and credit control and expansion, 112, 121, 125, 127–28
Depression, 18, 26, 28, 35
Direct loans: growth in number and value of, 3, 5, 7, 9, 23, 58, 60, 126, 127–28; subsidies in, 4, 13–15, 72, 138, 139, 142; provided by off-budget agencies, 4, 36–37, 38, 42, 58, 60, 72, 73–74, 75; and FFB, 7, 45, 56, 58, 60, 61, 87; defaults on, 12; economic effects of, 15; and loan guarantees, 26, 31, 50; nature and purpose of, 35–37; budgetary treatment of, 42, 45, 138, 139, 140, 142; as "bailout" credit, 79–80, 83, 87; efforts to control, 99–101, 107, 109–10, 120, 122, 123, 125, 131, 134–35; misestimation of in credit budget, 102, 110, 126; Reagan administration reductions in, 106, 110, 114, 115
Domenici, Pete, 33, 123

Economic Development Administration, 78
Education: credit assistance for, 3, 23, 29–33
Elementary and Secondary Education Act (1965), 30–31
Emergency Livestock Credit Act (1974), 65
Emergency Loan Guarantee Act (1970), 82
Emergency Loan Guarantee Board, 82
Emergency Rail Services Act (1970), 79
Energy development: credit assistance for, 23, 33–34, 71
Energy Security Act (1980), 75
Entitlement programs, 16, 23, 31, 94, 133
Environmental Financing Authority, 68, 154 (n. 6)
Exchange Stabilization Fund, 68
Executive branch, 16, 33, 105; and budget deficits, 10, 41; and credit policy and credit control, 19, 24, 37, 41, 53, 64, 89, 130, 141, 146; and FFB, 51; and Eximbank, 71; and REA, 75. See also individual administrations
Export-Import Bank (Eximbank): purpose and operations of, 36–37, 69–72; misestimation of activities of in credit budget, 102, 110; and Reagan budget, 110, 112, 114

Farm Credit Act (1933), 39
Farm Credit Administration, 38, 39, 67
Farmers Home Administration (FmHA), 28, 102; and loan asset sales, 7, 49–50, 56–58, 61, 73–74, 101, 115; and FFB, 7, 53, 56–58, 61–62; origin and purpose of, 35–36; and Reagan administration, 110, 115
Farm Security Administration, 35
Federal debt. See Deficit(s)
Federal Energy Regulatory Commission, 128
Federal Farm Loan Act (1916), 39
Federal Financing Bank (FFB), 39, 102, 126; and loan asset sales, 7, 45, 50, 51, 56–58, 61, 87, 101, 115–16, 125; purpose and operations of, 43–44, 51, 53–63; impact of, 43–44, 51–52, 54–63; establishment of, 50, 51, 53; and budgetary treatment of credit, 51–52,

56, 58–63, 107, 115–16, 125; off-budget status of, 68–69, 77; and credit control, 91, 95, 99, 100, 103, 125, 134–36, 157 (n. 24)
Federal Financing Bank Act (1973), 135
Federal Home Loan Bank Board, 67
Federal Home Loan Bank System, 37–38
Federal Home Loan Mortgage Corporation (FHLMC), 38–39, 67, 117, 161 (n. 35)
Federal Housing Administration (FHA), 13, 26–28, 115, 118
Federal Intermediate Credit Banks, 67
Federal Land Banks, 67
Federal National Mortgage Association (FNMA), 37–39, 48, 67, 117, 153 (n. 10), 161 (n. 35)
Federal Reserve Board, 90
Federal Ship Financing Act (1972), 65
Ford administration, 74, 83, 90–92, 104, 105

General Accounting Office (GAO), 13, 43, 49, 70, 90
Gorton, Slade, 150 (n. 27)
Government National Mortgage Association (GNMA), 28, 110, 112, 113, 115, 118
Government-sponsored enterprises: as impediment to credit policy and control, 19, 91, 93, 130, 145–46; purpose and operations of, 37–40, 77; exclusion of from unified budget, 65–68, 77, 91, 149 (n. 9), 154 (n. 5); and Reagan administration, 117–18, 146; and federal participation rate, 136
Great Plains Coal Gasification plant, 75–76
Guaranteed loans. See Loan guarantees

Hatfield, Mark, 122–23
Higher Education Act (1965), 30–31
Hoover Commission, 139–40
House of Representatives: Budget Committee, 37, 77, 90–91, 93, 98–99, 100, 101, 120, 121, 125, 132–33, 134, 137, 144, 145, 150 (n. 27); Banking Committee, 48, 49, 81–82, 83, 86, 98, 126, 128, 134, 136; Ways and Means Committee, 53; and Exim-bank, 70–71; Commerce Committee, 79; and "bailout" credit, 81–84, 86–87; Joint Study Committee on Budget Control, 88; Appropriations Committee, 93, 98, 100–101, 112, 123, 132, 144; Agriculture Committee, 98; Interior Committee, 98; Maritime Committee, 98; Small Business Committee, 98; Education and Labor Committee, 98, 126; and budget reform and credit control, 121–34 passim; Armed Services Committee, 127; Rules Committee, 132. See also Congress
Housing, 41–42, 94, 101, 109, 110, 131; as focus of federal credit assistance, 3, 16, 18, 23, 65; in spending budget, 18, 20; loan guarantees for, 23, 26, 28, 29; direct loans for, 23, 35; and government-sponsored enterprises, 38–39; and tax-exempt bonds, 40, 41; subsidies for, 104, 140
Housing for the Elderly and Handicapped Fund, 68, 101

Immigration and Naturalization Service v. Chadha, 135–36
Industrial development bonds. See Tax-exempt bonds
Interest rates: in federal credit programs, 4, 13–15, 26, 29, 31, 58, 74, 151 (n. 12); effect of credit programs on, 13–15, 34, 112; for government borrowing and securities, 38, 40, 52, 54; and interest subsidies, 140
Interstate Commerce Commission, 79

Johnson administration, 31, 46, 48–49, 61, 73

K Mart Corporation, 152 (n. 33)
Kudlow, Lawrence A., 117

Legislative veto, 135–36
Levin, Carl, 113
Loan asset sales, 38, 74; budgetary treatment of, 7, 43, 45, 46, 47–50, 56–58,
63; and FFB, 7, 50, 51, 56–58, 61; as
agency borrowing, 45, 47, 48, 49, 63,
92, 115; nature and utilization of, 47–
50
Loan guarantees: growth in number and
value of, 3, 4, 7, 19, 23, 46, 109–10,
126, 127–28, 152 (n. 25); defaults on,
4, 5, 12; assessing costs of, 4, 88,
138, 139; exclusion of from budget
process, 4–5, 9, 19, 45, 50–51, 62,
65, 88, 92, 149 (n. 9); subsidies in,
13–15, 29, 88, 138, 139, 140; economic effects of, 15, 110–12; illusory
costlessness of, 24, 33, 45, 83, 88,
127; and direct loans, 26, 50–51; in
actuarially sound programs, 26–28,
29, 151 (n. 8); for marginal borrowers,
29–33, 151 (n. 8); for technology development, 33–34; as alternative to direct spending, 34, 130; provided by
government-sponsored enterprises, 39;
accounting procedures for, 43, 45,
50–51, 58–60, 61, 63, 94; and FFB,
45, 56, 58–60, 61, 125; as "bailout"
credit, 79–83, 84, 85–87, 88; and
credit budget and credit control, 88,
91, 94, 97, 99–101, 107, 120, 122,
123, 125, 133–34, 142, 157 (n. 24);
misestimation of in credit budget, 102,
110, 114, 126; Reagan administration
reductions in, 106, 110–12, 113, 114,
115; impoundment of, 113, 135–36
Lockheed Corporation, 34, 65, 77, 79,
80–83, 85, 87–88, 127, 130
Lundine, Stan, 127

McIntyre, James T., 94–95
Maritime Administration, 78
Military sales, foreign: credit assistance
for, 35, 36–37, 58–60, 114
Mineta, Norman, 121, 131, 150 (n. 27)
Municipal Assistance Corporation, 83

National Consumer Cooperative, 110
National Defense Education Act (NDEA)
(1958), 29–30
National income accounts (NIA), 137
National Railroad Passenger Corpora-
tion. See Amtrak
National Rural Electric Cooperative As-
sociation, 36
New Deal, 18, 35, 36
New York City, 34, 77, 83–85, 87–88,
130
Nixon administration: and REA, 36, 72,
73, 74; and loan asset sales, 49; and
FFB, 53; and credit control, 64; and
Eximbank, 70; and "bailout" credit,
78, 80–81, 126–27

Off-budget agencies: direct lending by, 4,
37, 42; possible inclusion of in budget
process, 10, 88, 92, 104, 105, 134,
135, 136, 138; and on-budget agencies, 37, 69; Eximbank as, 49, 56, 68,
69–72; FFB as, 51, 58, 60, 62, 68–69;
growth in number and activity of, 64,
67, 68–69; government-sponsored enterprises as, 67–68, 77; funding and
operations of, 67–73, 154 (n. 6); REA
as, 68, 72–75, 152 (n. 25); and budget
deficit, 150 (n. 15)
Office of Management and Budget
(OMB), 12, 13, 53, 72, 90, 94–95,
112, 117–18, 139
Omnibus Budget Reconciliation Act
(1981), 65, 74, 76, 110
On-budget loans, 7, 9, 58, 135
O'Neill, Thomas P., 86

Packard, David, 81–82
Participation rate: of federal government
in credit market, 3, 10–11, 109, 136–
37
Participation Sales Act (1966), 48
Patman, Wright, 82
Pearson, James B., 132
Pell grants, 31, 33
Penn Central Transportation Company,

78–79, 80
Pension Benefit Guaranty Corporation, 68–69
Percy, Charles, 131
Postal Service Fund, 68, 76
President's Commission on Budget Concepts (Johnson administration), 46, 48–49, 50, 65–67, 70, 88, 140, 142, 147, 154 (n. 5)
Private purpose bonds. *See* Tax-exempt bonds
Proxmire, William, 71, 82, 137

Reagan administration, 12, 36, 53, 72, 74, 146; credit policy and credit budget of, 3, 64, 91, 106–19, 128, 129; spending policy and budget reforms of, 19–23, 106–19, 159 (n. 23); and loan asset sales, 63, 135
Reclamation Act (1902), 151 (n. 21)
Reconciliation Act (1980), 41
Reconstruction Finance Corporation, 18, 47–48, 127
Report of the Committee on Money and Credit (1961), 140
Rhyne, Elisabeth, 138
Ribicoff, Abraham, 132
Rivlin, Alice, 142
Rural Development Insurance Fund (of FmHA), 74
Rural Electrification Administration (REA): purpose and operations of, 36, 72–75; and Reagan administration, 36, 74, 110, 113, 115, 123; and loan asset sales, 49–50, 56–60; as off-budget agency, 68, 72–75, 152 (n. 25); and Congress, 72–75, 101
Rural Electrification and Telephone Revolving Fund, 112
Rural Environmental Assistance Program (REAP), 73
Rural Telephone Bank, 68, 72–75, 101

Senate: Budget Committee, 37, 77, 90–91, 93, 98, 99–100, 101, 120, 121, 132–33, 134, 137, 144, 145, 150 (n. 27), 157 (n. 24); Rules and Admin-
istration Committee, 50, 88; Banking Committee, 53, 70, 81–82, 84, 86, 134, 136; and Eximbank, 69–71; Commerce Committee, 79; and "bailout" credit, 81–84, 86–87; Joint Study Committee on Budget Control, 88; Appropriations Committee, 93, 98, 100–101, 112, 132, 144; and budget reform and credit control, 121, 123, 125, 127, 128, 131–34. *See also* Congress
Small Business Administration (SBA), 12, 29, 78, 110, 112, 113, 115
Small business: credit assistance for, 29, 33, 35
Spending: growth of, 3, 5, 16, 18, 19, 95, 102, 159 (n. 23); priorities in, 3, 19–23, 61, 100, 121, 124; compared with credit, 3–4, 11, 42, 44, 105, 118, 130; control efforts and mechanisms for, 3–4, 10, 16, 43, 91, 97–98, 100, 105, 120, 121, 132–34, 137, 146, 147; assessing costs of, 11, 44, 138–42, 145, 146; accountability for, 17; budget for compared with credit budget, 19, 23–26, 95, 102, 107–9, 114, 128, 129, 131; credit as alternative to, 29–31, 34, 43, 65, 88–89, 142–43, 145; budgetary treatment of, 43, 44, 46, 104, 130; and integration with credit in unified budget, 46, 138–42, 145, 146; and credit control, 91, 92, 97–98, 100, 105, 121, 135, 146; Reagan administration policy on, 106, 107, 110–11, 112, 113–14, 118, 120, 121, 125, 159 (n. 23); justification for and opposition to, 143–44
Staats, Elmer B., 70
Stockman, David, 86, 156 (n. 50)
Strategic Petroleum Reserve, 68, 69, 76
Student Loan Mortgage Association (SLMA), 38, 39, 67
Student loans, 34, 40, 102; defaults on, 12, 29, 33; interest rates and subsidies for, 13, 31, 151 (n. 12); origin and impact of, 29–33; and government-sponsored enterprises, 38, 39; and SLMA,

39, 67; and Reagan credit reductions, 106, 110, 115

Subsidies: providing of in federal credit programs, 4, 13–15, 28, 29, 31, 33, 34, 42, 72, 74–75, 79, 80, 105, 142; problems of measurement and budgetary treatment of, 5, 12, 46, 96, 138–40, 142, 144–45; for marginal borrowers, 29, 33, 34, 42; and tax-exempt bonds, 40–41; Reagan administration opposition to, 106, 110, 114, 115

Supreme Court, 135–36

Synthetic Fuels Corporation, 34, 69, 75–76

Tax-exempt bonds, 19, 38, 40–41, 44, 152 (n. 33)

Teeters, Nancy H., 24–26

Tennessee Valley Authority, 56

Transportation: credit assistance for, 20, 23

Treasury Department, 127; credit agency borrowing from, 36, 38, 44, 70, 74, 128, 154 (n. 6); and FFB, 51, 53, 54, 62; and government securities market, 52–53, 54

Unified budget. *See* Budget, federal

United Auto Workers, 85, 86

United States Railway Association (USRA), 68–69, 79–80

Vanik, Charles, 51, 71

Veterans Administration (VA), 28, 48, 115, 123

Volcker, Paul, 53

Washington Public Power Supply System (WPPSS), 128

Westinghouse Corporation, 37

Whitten, Jamie, 87

Wildavsky, Aaron, 131, 143, 144

Wright, Jim, 127